UNDYING WILL

UNDYING WILL

A FAMILY'S STORY OF SURVIVAL IN WAR TORN EUROPE

HARVY BERMAN

Dedicated to the memory of my parents, Nathan and Mira Berman, who did everything they could to leave the horrors of the Holocaust behind them.

CONTENTS

ACKNOWLEDGMENTS

WHEN MY HOPES OF MAKING A CAREER PLAYING football ended in 1974 due to back surgery, I decided to go into the family leather business. Nine o'clock breakfast, eleven o'clock schnapps, and twelve o'clock lunch were spent with uncles and cousins gathered around a large conference table. The business of the factory was discussed in a mix of English and Yiddish. Inevitably, the conversations would switch over to tales of my relatives' lives in Poland before and during the war. One day, my uncles were talking in Yiddish about my father's first wife. Unbeknownst to them, I had overheard their conversation and I realized I had just overheard a family secret. I wondered how much more of this time I was unaware. I began to take notes and ask questions. My notes sat for years while I helped run the family business, completed college, married, and raised a family. In 1992, when the family business was sold, I decided to pursue a lifelong dream in the martial arts. After meeting grandmaster

Helio Gracie in 1997, I could not get over how much he reminded me of my own father, who had passed away the previous year. It was at this time that I decided to dedicate the next part of my life in the study and teaching of Gracie Brazilian Jiu Jitsu.

In 2016, I received a call from an old family friend, Mark Upfall, whose father came from the same city in Poland as my father. He told me the story of Joe Gellman, another descendant of my family's city. Upon visiting his ancestor's gravesite in Kaluszyn, a barren field was all that greeted Joe, with no designation of what was once there. Joe and his friend, Ed Goldberg, began the long and arduous task of reclaiming the cemetery and creating a monument to honor the generations of Jews whose final resting space was desecrated by the Nazis, as well as the mass grave used to liquidate thousands of the town's Jews. I discovered that the land had been purchased and the monument, created by Israeli artist Ken Goldman, was being erected. In two months, there was going to be a dedication of which I was invited to attend.

Many thoughts crossed my mind as I recalled my father's words that he would never set foot in Poland again. My thoughts shifted to my grandparents, of whom I had never even seen a picture. I thought reciting Kaddish at the burial site of my grandparents, aunts, uncles, and half-brother would be a way to honor my parents and family. My wife, Jody, and I arrived in Warsaw and united with a few descendants of Kaluszyn. The next morning we drove to Kaluszyn to memorialize those long-forgotten souls. After the memorial and dedication service, we went on in search of my family's factory. Upon arriving, I was saddened to discover that the structure burned to the ground just two years prior. However, to my great surprise, we were able to locate the homes of my grandfather, Alter Pinchus, and Uncle Mendel. Walking in the footsteps of my family inspired me to get back to work and document my family story for my grandchildren and future generations. I took out my old notebook and realized I would need help in telling the story I had envisioned all these years. I was fortunate to come into contact with an old football friend, Brian Patterson, who always impressed me with his abilities as a multifaceted artist. We worked together for almost a year, and with Brian's help we were able to bring to paper that which I had only envisioned in my mind. I would like to express my gratitude to Sarah and David Waldshein—David for his translations from Yiddish to English of the Kaluszyn *safer*[1], and Sarah for her keen memory, recalling the many stories her mother, Ethel, had shared with her over the years. My Uncles Mendel and Joseph Berman for their firsthand account of our family story. One can only imagine the difficulty of putting into words and reliving the horrors they experienced. To my extended family, though I initially hoped to tell the stories of our entire family, I

---

[1]   After the destruction of the Jewish towns, survivors and descendants of the towns created a book, a *safer*, of each town, as a form of remembrance.

found the story of my father and old Sam's involvement in creating a soccer team in a small Jewish Shtetl to most resonate with me. To my wife, Jody, thank you for believing in me and supporting each endeavor and pursuit. To my daughters, Jaime and Aly, thank you for all your efforts, support, and encouragement throughout this process. Finally, to my grandchildren, Gianna, Vince, and Cece, this book is for you. Not so much to relive the horrors of the Holocaust, but to learn about the history, which is your heritage. Your ancestors' strength of character and fight for survival has been a great inspiration to me. My hope is that these stories of resilience and perseverance act as a reminder to you when faced with adversity.

It's not the strongest of the species that survives, nor the most intelligent that survives. It is the one most adaptable to change.

—CHARLES DARWIN

Nobody is born a warrior, in exactly the same way that nobody is born an average man. We make ourselves into one or the other.

—CARLOS CASTANEDA

The world will not be destroyed by those who do evil, but by those who watch them without doing anything.

—ALBERT EINSTEIN

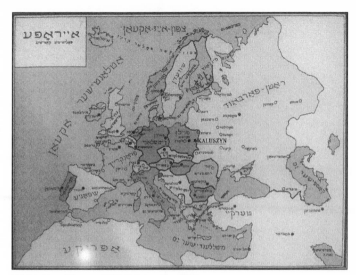

Yiddish Map of Europe, 1939. Note location of Kaluszyn.

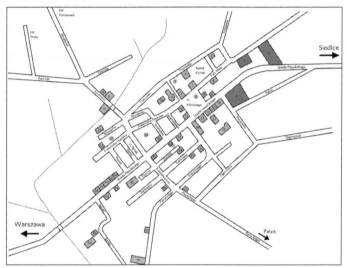

City Streets of Kaluszyn, 1938
1. New Jewish cemetery, founded between XIX-XX
2. Zwolinski's forge
3. Roman Catholic cemetery
4. Power Plant built in 1927 r.
5. Well at Trzcianka Street
6. Ms Wisniewska and Brzozowska's restaurant

7. City Council
8. Detka's forge
9. Berman and Guzik's tannery
10. Vicarage
11. Roman Catholic church built between 1890-1897
12. Primary school
13. Well at Kilinski Square (east side)
14. Police station
15. Commune office and the secretary Franciszek Frąckiewicz's house
16. Old Jewish cemetery
17. Jan Sieradzinski's tannery
18. No Data
19. Voluntary Fire Brigade Building
20. Post Office
21. Czerwiński Teofil Karol's forge
22. Natalia Rudzińska's restaurant (with jukebox)
23. Orphanage (location unsure)
24. Knife Manufacture; in 30' cinema "Uciecha"; part of first and the second floor inhabited by Jews
25. Mikvah, built around 1825 r.
26. Property of Stefan Kozlowski—chairman of Voluntary Fire Brigade; grocery store; most beautiful garden in town
27. Old mansion, partially inhabited by rabby Beniamin Michelson
28. Public well (108 m. of depth)
29. Karolina Roguska's restaurant
30. Stanislaw Nowak's restaurant
31. Well at the Stasiaka Street
32. Station of the narrow-gauge rail Kałuszyn—Mrozy
33. Grzegorz Kuc's forge
34. Tallith manufacture
35. Magistrate's court
36. Jewish hansom cab station (shuttling between Mrozy railway station and Kałuszyn)
37. No Data
38. M. Kisielnicki's restaurant
39. Teahouse
40. M. Kisielnicki's petrol making facility
41. I. Goldberg's petrol making facility
42. Two-story mill
43. Jewish forge (there were at least 3 of them)
44. Franciszek Klukowski's forge
45. Synagogue, destroyed by Germans in 1942, rabbi Shapiro's office, Jewish community house
46. No Data
47. Krzywoblocki's forge
48. Wooden house, veterinary office
49. No Data
50. Slaughterhouse
51. Nest's brewery

Great Synagogue of Kaluszyn, Destroyed 1939.

Kaluszyn early 1930s

Team Premium Soccer Club, Kaluszyn, 1930
Nathan Berman, second row, far left
Sam Berman (son of Motel), top row, third from left
Shia Berman (son of Yonkel), top left
Yosef Figenbaum, actual coach, top right
Additional teammates, unidentifiable. Yona Yedwab, Kochinik, Jacob Syzma, Jacob Susman,
Meyer Yangerzinski, Gadila Provila

Berman Factory, Kaluszyn, 1937
Sam Berman, far left
Nathan Berman, far right
Chaim Gutarsky, second from left

Nathan Berman, Warsaw, 1938

Nachema and Nathan Berman, Kaluszyn, 1938

BERMAN FAMILY TREE

FAMILY TREE FROM 1857 - 1961

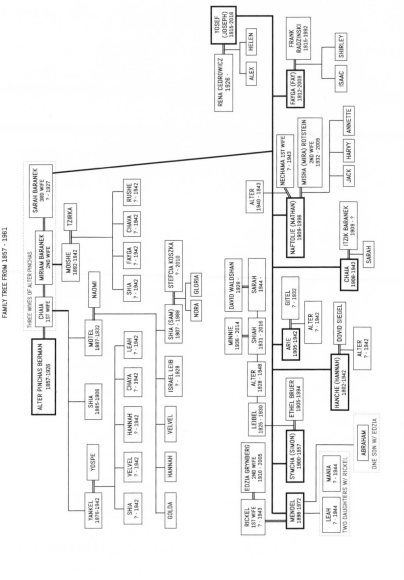

FOREWORD

"Although an estimated 80 percent of American Jews are of Polish descent, many in the postwar generation and those born later know little about their families' connection to their ancestral home."

THE CROOKED MIRROR: A MEMOIR OF POLISH-
JEWISH RECONCILIATION, KINDLE EDITION

BEFORE THE WAR, THERE WERE APPROXIMATELY 3.5 million Jews in Poland. After the war, there were somewhere between 50,000 and 120,000 survivors.

Most American Jews are directly connected to those survivors. It is amazing, however, how time impacts awareness and perception. The farther we are from the horrors of the Holocaust, the less it seems to factor in our lives.

And indeed, part of the triumph over such a horror is being able to move on and enjoy life. The survivors you will meet here embody that attitude and embraced life without being held captive by the terrible memories.

But it is important to remember and to understand how these Polish Jews managed to survive the Holocaust and arrive in the United States. Their stories tell of astonishing and heart-stopping experiences. Tattered black and white photographs and film clips don't tell the full story.

Fortunately, several survivors recorded their thoughts—stories of escape, survival, enduring love, starvation, mayhem, compassion, and murder with powerful firsthand accounts.

We are focusing on the stories told by the Berman family. Two members had their memories written down. Many others outside the family did the same, and we draw from those accounts on occasion, as well.

Our most important takeaway from these stories is not a catalogue of the atrocities, but it is an attempt to understand the strength and courage it took to never surrender—no matter what they faced or how long they had to endure it.

KALUSZYN, POLAND 1915–1945

Two autobiographical works, in the authentic voices of the authors, provide the vast majority of material that follows, with occasional notes to fill in additional perspective and quotes from the stories of others. The Berman autobiography authors, two of twelve siblings, are:

- Mendel Berman wrote *The Destruction of Kaluszyn*, translated from the original Yiddish by David Waldshan (1995). He is the nephew by marriage of the author. In his words, it is approximately 90 percent word for word and approximately 10 percent rephrased sentences due to some idiomatic Yiddish expressions. Mendel's work is included in the larger Memorial Book of Kaluszyn, first published in 1961 in Tel Aviv. Select additional quotes by other authors featured in that work are included herein on occasion and noted in the footnotes.

- Joseph Berman wrote an *Autobiography of a Survivor*. This diary is longer and more comprehensive, and so provides most of the narrative contained herein. Joseph continued his remembrances beyond the Holocaust years and into the times when the family emigrated to new worlds.

The chapters recounting their Holocaust experiences (1939–1945) tell amazing stories: How five of the Bermans, after jumping off the death train headed to Treblinka, held together for nearly three years in the rugged countryside of Kaluszyn narrowly escaping certain death at every turn, desperately trying to keep the family alive and intact. (Two more in this group also escaped the Nazis, but later succumbed to disease.)

Kaluszyn was a small "shtetl" or town. Some 80 percent of its residents were Jews. As those five Bermans returned to Kaluszyn once the Nazis had been routed, they found that there were only a total of about ten Jews left in the ruined town, out of more than 8,000 before the war.

Shortly after the war, they were rejoined by six more family members who escaped the fate at Treblinka and survived in Russia, with their own harrowing survival stories including banishments to Siberia.

After the war, another journey would then begin that led to the United States.

This was a large family. Sometimes, there are more than a few members bearing the same first name. It can get confusing to track. A family tree is included in the pictorial section to clarify who is who.

Additional chapters interspersed throughout the book recount the experiences of the Berman family prior to the outbreak of the German invasion of Poland in 1939. These stories come from your author's recollection of family discussions over the past forty years.

We wanted to look at this particular time because this was a period of relative peace and prosperity following and just prior to especially violent and traumatic periods of Polish history. A bubble in time—a few years after the German invasion of World War I and the subsequent Soviet invasion that lasted until March 1921. And it was some thirteen years prior to the start of World War II and the Nazi horrors.

It was in this time frame that young Nathan Berman,

seventeen, was, in fact, appointed head of the family business after the death of the patriarch, Alter Pinchus Berman. Nathan was a fun-loving youth, known to enjoy cigarettes and vodka. He was not strictly orthodox, much like his beloved father, Alter.

Nathan and several relatives and friends did indeed play on a soccer team in the town. Team Premium is believed to be the first organized team to ever come from a predominantly Jewish shtetl (town).

The soccer stories also feature a Polish Catholic boy named Stanislaw Boruc. Boruc played a crucial role in the family's survival during the Holocaust. However, his involvement in the soccer team is plausible fiction.

For their efforts in sheltering the Bermans and others during the Holocaust, Boruc and his wife, Teofila, were awarded by the Institute Yad Vashem in Jerusalem with the title "Righteous Among Nations."

Since it is a known fact that Stanislaw Boruc and Nathan Berman's fathers were indeed good friends in real life, we took the leap to imagine the two sons may have played a sport together. So, it's not such a huge leap.

It is also worth noting that the coach of the team, Bela Sebesteyn, was actually a Jewish soccer star who played for Hungary in the Olympics. There were perhaps a couple dozen Jewish soccer players of note in the entire world in this era. When inventing a coach for the team, we decided to honor Bela's name and his real-world accomplishments.

We tell these stories as best we can based on historical facts about Kaluszyn, the rapidly evolving Jewish culture of those times, some cherished family anecdotes, and some fanciful imaginings when it comes to the soccer games.

The stories are intended to try and help us understand the mental outlook on life and spiritual strength that must have developed in those who never quit fighting to survive the Nazi horrors—regardless of the danger and overwhelming odds against them.

Watching loved ones marched off to be murdered... Escaping a death train by blindly leaping out a small vent opening...Surviving the harsh outdoor elements, living in holes in the ground...Hunted at every turn by Polish bounty hunters, German army, SS, gestapo...Shot, starving, cold, wet, hungry, and on full alert twenty-four hours per day.

And this went on for nearly three years.

How did they find the strength to keep going, to survive?

One continues to wonder. When you read their stories of survival, you will likely be left marveling at the same question. It is virtually impossible for those of us who did not experience these terrors to truly understand how it felt. And how, after suffering repeated blows to mind and body, anyone could continue getting back up again and again?

We've done our best to try and understand how

Nathan Berman and the others managed to do it. Trying to imagine their formative years was one way to try and understand how their outlook on life may have developed. To say the family was tight-knit is an understatement. They were woven together by unbreakable bonds that evolved naturally in their way of life in the shtetl.

So, it is worth trying to understand the times before the Holocaust and the influences that helped inspire such strong spirits and the resolve to fight for family.

In that same spirit, Nathan Berman often said in his later years in America when confronted with a difficult challenge. With a broad smile across his face, he would say, "Hitler could not kill me, so why should I be afraid?"

CHAPTER ONE

AUTOBIOGRAPHY OF A SURVIVOR, JOSEPH BERMAN, PART I

Kaluszyn, 1915

"I WAS BORN ON DECEMBER 15, 1915 DURING WORLD War I in a small town called Kaluszyn, located fifty-six kilometers east of Warsaw. Kaluszyn lies on the main road between Warsaw and Moscow. I was the youngest child of my father's third wife. My father had twelve children: nine boys and three girls. Eight of them were from my mother (Sarah).

When I was born, I was an "instant" uncle. My oldest brothers already had children in their late teens, and on their own. At the age of four or five, I started Hebrew school, where we learned the daily prayers as well as the Torah.

At the age of seven, I was also enrolled in the public school. I attended the Hebrew classes in the morning and public school in the afternoon, till 5 p.m. As a result, I was quite busy the entire day, with very little time to play. Besides, we really had nothing to play with.

The only sport was soccer. My favorite subjects in school were reading and writing (Polish of course), geography and astronomy.

The school years seemed to pass quickly. Economically, things during World War I and the years that followed, were not so good. I remember Polish farmers bringing their raw lambskins to my father. He processed them, and later made them into sheepskin coats. In exchange, the farmers would give him live chickens, eggs, butter, cheese, and grain.

I recall one room which always had loose grain all over the floor. This was because the farmers wanted to take their burlap bags back home with them, so they just emptied the grain on the wooden floor.

All this must have occurred during World War I and the first years after Poland became independent.

I remember on one occasion, being carried on the shoulders of my brother, Arie, who was about ten years older than I, to the main road between Warsaw and Moscow, which crossed our town. There I saw, what I later learned was the Soviet Red Army cavalry marching through our city toward Warsaw. Poland was at war with Bolshevik Russia. The Polish army, with the help of the French, managed to push the Red Army from Polish territory.

NOTE: The Russians invaded after the end of WWI in 1918 and were gone by 1921, leading to a period of Polish independence that lasted up until the Nazi invasion of 1939.

There was very little school during the time the Russians occupied Poland. This lasted several centuries. During World War I, which lasted from 1914 to 1918, when the Germans occupied the country, the schools were closed most of the time. After the peace treaty was signed in Versailles in 1918, the Western Allies granted independence to Poland.

"My memories of my parents are few. My father, Alter Pinchus, was a tall, strong man with a gray beard. I recall him getting up early each morning and bringing hot bagels to us children while we were still in bed. He was a hardworking man, working fourteen to sixteen hours per day, six days a week, trying to support a large family. I can remember being spanked only once, with a leather strap.

I must have been five or six years old. It was at the time the sport of soccer took hold in our town, and everyone was kicking anything that would roll. I was kicking a round stone on my way back from Hebrew school and was wearing new shoes.

This was something not everyone could afford. To my surprise, my father was behind me all the time, and that was the reason I was spanked for ruining my shoes.

But around a year later we had a real soccer ball at home, and my father let me kick it all the time.

My father was not very orthodox, but he was a very traditional man. On Saturdays, he would take me along to the synagogue, and after the services we would come home to a good Shabbat dinner.

My mother was always busy cooking, mending socks, and doing the laundry; all by hand because there weren't any washing machines or dryers. The laundry had to dry outside in the summer or in the attic during the winter. She was a wonderful cook. Every Thursday night she would bake for the Sabbath. I would stay up till past midnight, so I could eat some warm rolls.

I remember the excitement when a wealthy Jewish family that my father knew from Warsaw named Hoffenberg came to visit us. They talked to my father about a joint partnership to bid for a government contract to supply the Polish army and the railroad department with warm sheepskin coats.

Our joint bid was successful, and a government inspection was expected. Since our house was used as our working place, all of our furniture and other personal belongings were removed to other locations to impress the inspectors that our home was actually a factory. We got the okay to go ahead and start.

Times were rapidly changing. Lots of people were hired to help meet the heavy schedules demanded by the contract. Economically, things began to improve. Year

after year, our bids for government contracts were successful in spite of tough competition.

CHAPTER TWO

ALTER PINCHUS PASSES AWAY

Kaluszyn, Poland, February 1926

ALTER PINCHUS BERMAN WAS AN IMPOSING FIGURE, standing over six feet tall, with a full head of hair and a neatly trimmed graying beard. He was respected and admired by his family and townspeople, Jew and gentile alike. He was known for his strong hands, quick wit, and keen desire for honesty and fairness.

Once, one of the young Berman boys made some snide, unflattering remarks toward an elderly woman. The woman quickly made her way to the home of Alter Pinchus to explain what had happened and to see the young boy properly punished.

"I understand that my young son made some remarks that were entirely inappropriate," Alter said to her. "Tell me, what did you do after he made these remarks?"

"I slapped him across his face!"

"Well then, it seems to me that his punishment has already been delivered. I think it would be inappropriate for me to punish the young boy twice for the same crime."

It was common for the Berman family to all come together at Alter's home. The gatherings were quite extensive, with twenty to thirty family members coming by regularly to eat and interact. Food was spread across the large wooden table, and a lively discussion ensued. Alter always encouraged even the youngest in attendance to take part in the discussions, valuing open debate. All topics were fair game.

But on this particular evening, there was a stillness across the home. Instead of a lively discussion on the political, economic, and religious ramifications of the recent Russian Revolution, tonight's focus was the health of the family patriarch.

Tonight there would be no lessons from the great sage of the Berman family. Alter was in bed, sweating profusely. Two years prior, the family gathered with similar circumstances, thinking the end was near. Some even began to pray in hopes of a miracle. Their prayers were heard. Alter fought off death on that day and the family gathered again, this time for a huge celebration. Alter quickly resumed his role at the factory. However he realized that his health was declining. He had a big decision to make: who would take over the leadership responsibilities of the factory upon his demise?

Nathan was hard at work cutting the fine shearling hides into long coats that would warm the Polish military and railroad workers. As Alter approached young Nathan, he was certain which of his twelve children would be best suited to take over his duties at the factory. "Nathan, how is the production going?" he asked.

"We have a large order for the railroad due to ship next week. We will need to work overtime and into the weekend to get it done, but I see no problem."

"No problem for you," little Chaimel yelled out from his sewing station. Chaim Gutarsky was a nephew of Alter's second and third wives. "Work, work, work. We work longer hours and get paid the same. Thanks to the Communist revolution in Russia, this form of production and capitalism will soon be outlawed."

"Chaimel," Alter raised his voice, "tell me, what will happen to your father's Cheder and our great synagogue when your beloved Communists come marching into town?"

"You Bermans, always supporting the bourgeoisie," Chaimel replied.

Nathan, with a smile on his face, interrupted. "Thank you for all your efforts, Chaim, we appreciate your service to our company."

Chaim waved his hand and returned to work. Alter turned to Nathan. "Come to the kitchen."

Alter poured a cup of tea for himself and sat down at the table. "I have noticed how dedicated you are to the factory," he told Nathan. "Your efforts are appreciated. When my time comes, and I am laid to rest, I want you to take over my position and duties at the factory."

"What about my older brothers?" Nathan asked.

"Their interests lie in other areas. You, my son, are best suited for this position. Work hard, meet a nice girl, get married, and enjoy your life. Things will work out fine, I promise."

Nathan did not hesitate. "Of course, my father, I will always obey your wishes and do my best to make you proud."

Now, Nathan and his seven brothers all gathered in Alter's bedroom, hoping for another miracle. But not on this day. Alter took a deep breath, a peacefulness radiated from his pale face, and the end was here.

"Baruch Dayan Ha'emet, blessed be the true judge," the men recited in unison. Symcha approached the now lifeless body and closed Alter's eyes and mouth, then pulled the sheet up to cover his face. The brothers placed the covered body on the floor. Alter's wife, Sarah, entered the room, placing candles near her husband's head. As she lit the candles, the family began to recite Psalm 23: "The Lord is my shepherd..." After they recited King David's words, silence filled the room.

The rabbi was summoned and arrangements were made for the funeral the following morning. In the meantime, Alter's sons would act as Shemira (honor guard), taking turns watching over the body to comfort the soul which, according to scripture, would not ascend to heaven until the body was laid in its final resting space.

The funeral was held in the bitter cold, early the next morning. But that cold weather couldn't keep the people of our city from attending. Jews and gentiles lined the street to honor Alter Pinchus, respected by all, a pillar of the community. According to the religious rules of those days, the sons of the departed had to be at the cemetery early. They could see from far away half of the city's population following the casket of their father, which in those days, men carried on their shoulders. Alter's wife and four daughters were seated. As the coffin was lowered into the earth, his nine sons stood and recited the Mourners Kaddish.

Alter Pinchus Berman died of pneumonia at the age of sixty-nine. After seven days of mourning, everyone picked up his or her duties. Fay and Joseph went back to school, while Arie, Hannah, and Chaya resumed working in the shop. Nathan, seventeen years old at the time, took over father's duties at the factory.

CHAPTER THREE

AUTOBIOGRAPHY OF A SURVIVOR, PART II

Kaluszyn, 1927

AFTER MY FATHER DIED, MY MOTHER WAS CON-stantly sick, and only eleven months later, she also died. It was January of 1927. Hannah took over the duties of my mother, as she was the oldest. She was twenty-four years old at that time. About eighteen months later she got married, and sister Chaya took her place at the age of nineteen.

"I remember it was the end of 1928 and I was twelve years old. I had my Bar Mitzvah at twelve because according to Jewish law, if you are an orphan, your Bar Mitzvah has to be at twelve years. In those days, nobody had a big party for a Bar Mitzvah. I remember I was given a bottle of vodka and a sponge cake. I took them to the synagogue, and they called me to the Torah and I said the mafter.

After the services, everybody took a glass of vodka and a piece of sponge cake, and they wished me the best, and that was my Bar Mitzvah.

In that year, we bought a piece of land adjacent to our property, and we built a new three-story, brick factory. I joined the Zionist Youth Organization at that time. We met on weekends for all types of activities, like celebrating all the Jewish holidays by going out on marches through the woods, and other exercises.

At the end of 1929 through 1930 there was a setback in the economy throughout Europe, including Poland. It also affected our business; we received very few orders, and people blamed it on the Depression in America. We had to lay off most of our workers, because we had to buy our raw material in Balkan countries with US dollars, and the dollar went up from five zloty to nine zloty.

We did get paid from the Polish government with zloty, so our raw material almost doubled and we took a beating. To fill the gap in 1931, our company leased one of the largest apple orchards in Poland, which was located in our area.

At the same time, my sister Fay and I had finished public school. I enrolled in a trade school in Warsaw which was fifty-six kilometers from Kaluszyn. We had to pay for school, room, and food.

It was the first time I had ever left home. At home, business was bad. They were losing money in the apple orchards, and the sheepskin coat business was still very slow. I felt that I was putting an economic burden on my family, so after one year at trade school, I quit and went home to help.

I was then sixteen years old. I started to work in the factory. At first, I learned the whole process of tanning the skins and making them into garments. I was working at least ten hours a day. In the evenings, I would go out with my friends to the boardwalk on the main street which was called Warsaw Street. There we met with girls from our Zionist Youth Organization, and we spent the evenings together.

CHAPTER FOUR

THE AGE OF JEWISH ENLIGHTENMENT

Kaluszyn, 1929

THEY HAD NO WAY OF KNOWING IT, BUT LIFE WAS an off-the-grid struggle in Kaluszyn. There were no streetlights, central water distribution, or sewage system in town. People hauled water from the river or a nearby well that belonged to a non-Jew. These hardships were simply normal, everyday life.

Near the river stood the remains of the old burned-down synagogue that had served the people for hundreds of years. Many people believed it was haunted. Superstitions ran rampant. Many feared the spirits living in the ruins of the synagogue and in the river itself. Exorcists often sold their services to the jittery residents of Kaluszyn.

Housing conditions for the most part were poor. Almost all the houses and buildings in town were made of wood. Jews who lived in apartments usually had only two or three rooms among them.

In spite of being in Poland since the Middle Ages, Jews were not assimilated into the broader Polish population. Before WWI, the town was quite backward culturally. There were few schools.

Shtetl towns like Kaluszyn were encircled by Catholic villages and estates. The market place was in the center of town and this is where the gentiles would come to buy goods.

Young rebellious people like the boys would have struggled to get by in those times. Then, the young had very little social freedom. For a young man and woman to meet unescorted, they would have to separately sneak away to Warsaw Street, which was the unofficial meeting place for young lovers.

The town did greatly benefit from its geographic location, midway between the big city of Warsaw and the eastern Polish border. This also brought lots of trouble over the centuries as it was considered a strategic military asset. Some of the older residents claim they can recall when Napoleon's army came marching through town on its way to Moscow. During World War I, it was the Germans who were unwelcome invaders, followed shortly thereafter by the Russian Cossacks on horseback.

After World War I and after the Russian invaders left in 1921, things changed. The Germans had been harsh on matters of economics, but liberal in terms of culture.

Following an end to all this warfare, there was an explosion of academic and intellectual interest. Newly independent, the Polish constitution granted equality to all citizens. A Jewish scientific institute was established to document Jewish culture and the Yiddish language (that continues today as the YIVO Institute for Jewish Research in New York).

Several schools and libraries opened in Poland through the cultural associations that sprang up. One of these, the Bund, also established a sports club called Morgenstern. It was from within it that Nathan and Sam's Team Premium developed.

And in 1926, Józef Piłsudski seized power in Poland. He was a strong opponent of anti-Semitism. This provided protection and some peace of mind for Poland's Jews and earned him the nickname "Grandpa." At this time, Jews made up about 10 percent of the entire Polish population.

Poland has a very long Jewish history. Scholars estimate that by the sixteenth century, 80 percent of all the Jews in the world lived in Poland. Rich Jewish cultural movements first evolved in this area of Europe.

Some historians have described Poland as "the paradise of Jews" at certain points in history. Jewish people called the country "Polin," which in Hebrew means "rest here" or "there you shall dwell."

In part, this is because Poland was the only country to accept a massive influx of Jewish immigrants when they fled the terror of the Christian Crusades.

The largest numbers of Jews migrated to Poland during the fourteenth and fifteenth centuries. They came mostly from Germany, Austria, and Hungary. These were Ashkenazi Jews, as opposed to Sephardic Jews who were prevalent in faraway Southern Europe, in places like Portugal and Spain.

Even as far back as the early twelfth century, there are signs of the presence of Jews in Poland. For example, a carving on the front door of the oldest Polish cathedral shows a scene of Jews, and there are even Hebrew words on very old Polish coins.

The Jewish people were known as expert traders, traversing all over the world to buy furs, grains, and spices to sell in the market squares, the main place that Jews and gentiles would mingle. When trade became difficult, Jews turned to trades like cobblers, blacksmiths, millers, and so on.

MIGRATION AND EUROPEAN CULTURE: ORIGINS OF JEWS IN POLAND

It was here in Poland that the mystic Hasidism originated. And in the 1920s, the Jewish cultural reform movement known as Haskalah took hold. The Berman boys were natural outgrowths of this movement: an evolving type of Jewish person was emerging.

The Haskalah is often seen as the Jewish version of the Age of Enlightenment. They championed liberal thinking and intellectual curiosity. Among them were radicals who argued for major changes in Jewish culture and life.[2]

And while Nathan and Sam were too young to be considered leading-edge thinkers or radicals, their attitudes toward life fit right in with this new cultural outlook. The boys remained fiercely devoted to family and upholding their responsibilities in the factory. But, at the same time, they believed in having a good time.

And rather than shelter away from the rest of the world, they believed "what's wrong with taking the others on in a friendly game of soccer?"

For many of their contemporaries, the idea of playing soccer against teams of goyim was crazy and absolutely out of the question, especially since games were held on the Shabbat.

"My head is fercockt," Nathan moaned as he let out a long plume of smoke.

"Man begins in dust and ends in dust," his nephew Sam replied, but in Yiddish, quoting an expression their fathers often used. "Meanwhile, it's good to drink some vodka."

Nathan and Sam rolled to the ground trying to suppress their laughter. It would be unwise to draw attention to themselves this morning. Not just yet, anyway.

Nathan and his nephew Sam were bad boys.

---

2   Wikipedia, s.v. "Haskalah," last modified February 28, 2019, https://en.wikipedia.org/wiki/Haskalah.

These boys were shedikers, Yiddish for trouble-makers. They were not malicious or evil, but definitely rebellious and out of sync with the town's more devout residents. While just about everyone else was in Shul on this Shabbat morning, Nate and Sam were nursing mild hangovers and sneaking smokes in the shed behind the family's factory.

Sam was technically Nate's nephew, but they were close in age and acted like brothers. They were members of the Berman family, which was known for its large numbers—Nathan was one of twelve siblings. The family was best known for its successful business making shearling coats.

Many other Kaluszyn boys their age were Hasidic Jews. They wore hats and "payot" sidelocks of hair. Older men wore long beards. Nathan and Sam wore haircuts similar to goyim Polish boys—nothing elaborate or special. They were not against religion by any stretch, but it did not define every aspect of life for them.

On this early morning, the boys could've used some coffee, as well. Last night, they had maybe a little too much vodka. But there was no time for wallowing. This was the day they had been waiting for, for many months. It was the first match for Team Premium—the first Jewish team to ever compete in Polish District soccer.

Nate and Sam believed this would be an epic day in many respects. After all, they were the best players on

Team Premium. Each of them would no doubt score many goals, just as they regularly did in practice against their teammates.

Confident? "Ay-Yay-Yay!"

That day, they would become legends.

For the moment though, they smoked in the shed praying their heads would stop pounding. Like most of the buildings in town, the Berman home was made of wood and vulnerable to fires.

Nathan's vision to build a brick building to house the business was completed. A great brick building, three stories tall!

In Nathan's mind, the brick factory would stand as a monument to his father, Alter, who started the business many years ago.

Jews were largely restricted from owning land, so they could not be farmers like the vast majority of Poles. They could not work civic jobs as on the railroads, and very few held jobs as teachers. Small trades and craftsmanship, like the Berman's trade making shearling coats, did not require owning large tracts of land and this is how most Jews earned their livelihoods.

The Bermans were devout capitalists and worked around the restrictions and obstacles to grow a profitable business. Alter was a dynamic force respected by Jews and non-Jews alike.

Nathan tried to model himself after his father, who was not very orthodox, but did respect religious and cultural tradition. Nathan, perhaps, in his youth was even a bit less orthodox at times.

His new responsibility was enormous, but Nathan relished it. He had boundless energy and a sharp mind. He tried to memorize every ounce of wisdom his father had shared as they worked side by side. With such a large and supportive family, Nathan never felt alone or at odds with his siblings.

Everyone knew how fortunate all of them were to have this prosperous business. The business was the family and family made the business.

The streets all around were dirt. On that day, they were thick with mud from the previous night's rain. The mud splashed wildly when a horse-drawn wagon rolled through. Of course, there were no wagons rolling this early morning. Nothing and nobody stirred, except Nathan and Sam.

Kaluszyn was located along the main road between Warsaw and Siedlice that led to Brest and the eastern border of Poland. Given its location, shipments of goods to and from the big market in Warsaw streamed through the little town.

On Fridays and Sundays, Jewish suppliers and merchants loaded up the carts and trucks with goods—chickens, dairy, and other manufactured goods—headed to Warsaw. Loud and hectic, the loading days were boisterous as merchants haggled for hours with drivers over rates. The situation repeated on

Tuesdays and Fridays when the carts would return and merchants crawled all over the drivers to learn what sold and at what price.

Each merchant's livelihood depended on the success of these trips.

NOTE: We quote here from a chapter in *The Memorial Book of Kałuszyn: Kałuszyn—Our Town* by Shalom Soroka.

Two Markets—the Old Market and Horse Market

The commercial center was the old market located in the center of Kałuszyn. For generations Jews struggled here to earn a living and continue their physical existence. The old homes that were about to crumble testified to the daily struggle of the Jews.

...In the middle of the market stood the big night oil lamp that was lit every night and provided a shady light on the stone covered ground of the market. From this area a ways down was the race area for the youngsters who drove their four wheeled carts, and in the winter this was the local scene of winter sports where the youngsters used their sleds and ice skates. There was an old water well in the market with a chain attached pail. It was later replaced with a pump.

"The market was surrounded with one or two story houses that contained stores with a great variety of merchandise...

...The market was a real show of colors and scents. Here the wholesalers, retailers, the big and small merchants, the vendors competed for sales. The crowd consisted of well to do buyers and people that barely finished the day. Some stores were busy beehives while others awaited the customer..."

...The Jewish character of Kałuszyn gave the Jews a sense of security that enabled them to withstand all the pressures and anti-Jewish laws that were enacted against them from the Czarist period down to the Polish period of the thirties. The Kaluszyner Jewish community knew how to defend itself, especially the working elements and the youth against any lurking dangers and attacks by Polish underworld gangs even physically when needed.

In those moments we saw the entire Jewish community standing united regardless of religious or secular affiliations facing their opponent. This idea of the united stand was carried over to the daily worries for the continuation of Jewish existence in Kaluszyn. Although each element was concerned with its own people be it Hasidim, secular, Zionists, or workers, there was still an overall concern for the existence of the Jewish character of Kaluszyn.

The old market remained the commercial center of Jewish Kałuszyn where the mass protests, worker demonstrations and election rallies took place. The old houses of the old market witnessed the growth of the Jewish working movement fighting for their rights...[3]

And so this was life in the town of Kaluszyn. The town was rustic in many ways, but also brimming with life.

The success the Bermans were enjoying could have easily bred contempt within the family. It can breed competition and petty jealousies. Success can tear a close-knit family apart.

The Bermans wisely enacted a rule to guard against this, and it would serve them well for generations to come. All business talk was left on the shop floor. None of the day-to-day tensions or passionate arguments could be brought home to the dinner tables. None of it. Ever.

In this way, wives and other family members were buffered from the business pressures. Common disagreements were not given the breathing room to grow into larger disputes with everyone taking sides.

The business was the family and the family was the business. But it was kept within the factory. Family bonds grew even stronger as a result. The Bermans were a very tightly knit group of people.

Life was good in 1929.

---

3   Shalom Soroka, trans. William Leibner, *The Memorial Book of Kaluszyn: Kaluszyn—Our Town* (Tel Aviv: 1961).

CHAPTER FIVE

GAME DAY

Kaluszyn, 1930

TODAY WAS GAME DAY.

The boys left the shed and hurried back to their respective homes to grab breakfast with the family. Then, it was off to the market square where a transport was arranged to take the entire team on the thirty-five-mile journey to Warsaw and the big match.

As the chattering boys gathered and clambered into the truck, Nathan was surprised to see a crowd gathering around them. He knew they were not supporters of the team, but he did not expect what happened next.

"Oy gevalt!" shouted one visibly angry man, shaking his fist at the boys as he tried to restrain his language in deference to the Shabbat.

"Chillul-Hashem!"

Several in the crowd chanted, calling out the sacrilege of disobeying the Shabbat.

The grandmother of the family that lived next door to Sam was more creative, pointedly calling out the Kaluszyn boy's relatively small stature in a mocking singsong.

"You schmendricks will be made fools by those giant goyim," she jeered repeatedly.

Her insult stung most.

After all, the players on Team Premium were somewhat short in stature, like most Jews of the time. While Sam and his uncle Arie were close to six feet. Most of the boys were in the five-foot-plus range in height. But the Polish goyim were legendary for their tall stature and blond hair.

The boys, though, often joked that the Poles were too clumsy and lumbering to contend with the talent of Team Premium. Nathan mused to himself: "Now, this grandmother is cursing us, saying we're small and that the giants will crush us?"

Nathan drifted into deep thought. He saw himself running circles around giant Poles. He was able to tune out most of the insults the crowd continued to hurl at the team.

"Giants?" Nathan thought.

"So what? Don't these devout people know what we Jews do with giants?

"Didn't Moses slay Og? Didn't David slay Goliath?"

"Ha. Wait and see what we do with these giants."

It was then the first stone landed, glancing harmlessly

just to the left of Nathan's aching head. It jolted him back to the present reality. His own townsfolk were stoning them!

"Geyn!" Nathan yelled at the driver to go.

"Geyn! Before these crazy people kill us."

The transport lurched forward and quickly left the angry crowd behind, splashing them with a wave of mud for good measure. This, of course, made them even angrier, but that did not matter for now. The stones soon fell short and stopped.

The rumble of the transport drowned the insults out. Nathan and the boys soon put the venom of their neighbors out of mind and focused on the match.

Team Premium was well on its way to Warsaw, where the first Jewish soccer team in Polish District history would score the first of many epic victories to come. Each of them had been anticipating this moment for months. No one could rob them of it.

As the wagons rolled over the Lover's Lane Bridge to Warsaw, Nathan urged his teammates on with a little humor and some bravado. He was, of course, team captain and their leader. It was his responsibility to put their minds on the game.

"Bring these giants on," Nathan exhorted.

"I will sling the ball into the goal over and over again until they are vanquished!"

The team laughed and cheered.

Then Nathan led them in several rounds of the ancient

Hebrew battle cry, a ritual they repeated before each practice. And now before the first game.

Nathan loudly asked the team, "Rak?"

"Can we be this?"

They replied,

"Chazak Amats!"

"Be strong, stand firm with courage and fear not!"

"Rak?"

"Chazak Amats!!!"

CHAPTER SIX

THE FIRST SOCCER MATCH VS. TEAM MAZZOVIA

Warsaw, 1930

HAPPILY, THE BOYS HAD MANAGED TO KEEP THEIR breakfasts in their stomachs as the transport finally lurched to a halt at the soccer pitch in Warsaw.

As they surveyed the playing field, some were intimidated straight away. For one thing, this field appeared to be lush grass and not the hardscrabble dirt back home.

But more importantly, the Polish boys of Team Mazzovia really were big. They wore nice uniforms and entered the field like a well-trained military unit. They executed crisp synchronized movements as they circled their end of the field, shouting their team's battle cry to intimidate the boys.

"Na wroga!" they chanted repeatedly in deep-voiced unison.

"On the Enemy!" in Polish.

Meanwhile, Team Premium, with its homemade jerseys and lack of choreography, meekly crept onto the field. Nathan was oblivious to his teammates' trepidations. He didn't care if the other guys had better uniforms and a slick pregame routine.

This was about soccer.

Then the catcalls began from the Polish team's many supporters lining the sidelines.

"Christ killers!"

"Jews go home!"

And much worse.

Some Poles had become less tolerant of Jews in these times. Anti-Semitism fueled by nationalism was fomenting elsewhere in Europe and creeping into Poland itself. An undercurrent of ugliness was growing.

Compounding matters on this day, Team Premium did not have a coach. As captain, Nathan served as their leader. He chose who played where and gave the pregame instructions. He pulled the twelve boys into a huddle and tried to make light in hopes of calming their nerves.

"At least they're not throwing rocks like our own neighbors. Just don't listen to them," Nathan attempted to joke.

"But Nathan," Arie, his older brother by four years interjected, "we are clearly overmatched. It's not just how big they are. They have great experience at this game. We're doomed."

"We're just as good as they are," Nathan snapped back. "We can play with them. We can beat them!"

And so the game began. Team Premium played with heart, at least at first, but they had little else going for them.

The referees kept control and the game went smoothly, for the Polish team. Unfortunately, the boys from Kaluszyn were indeed no match for this formidable Warsaw group. The Poles had been playing together for many years, not mere weeks. They won easily, 15 - 0.

Adding insult to the tough loss, the boys from Kaluszyn were sent away from the field with more catcalls and worse—derisive laughter that mocked their pathetic play.

"Look at the little Jew boys, they all chase the ball together like chicks chasing a mother hen," one heckler shouted.

"They have no business playing soccer; why have they wasted our time? This was not even a worthwhile practice," another chimed in.

And of course, the vicious catcalls insulting their religion and culture continued. It went on like this until the boys climbed back into the truck for the long ride back to Kaluszyn.

On the ride in, joyful banter and Nathan's boastful encouragement drowned out the racket of the road. Now though, the boys remained silent as the truck creaked and groaned.

Even Nathan.

As they entered Kaluszyn, they were greeted with another volley of stones and angry accusations. The religious quarter remained furious over the desecration of the Shabbat. Insults heaped atop injuries.

The boys lost badly on all fronts. The humiliation was devastating and complete. Nathan couldn't bring himself to say it out loud, but in his heart he believed they would regroup tomorrow at practice. They would learn from this loss, make changes, become better.

"Just wait," Nathan thought.

CHAPTER SEVEN

COACH BELA

Kaluszyn, 1930

PRACTICE HAD BEEN SCHEDULED FOR THE NEXT day following Team Premium's humiliating loss in Warsaw. But only five of the team's dozen players showed up.

"Where is everyone?" Nathan yelled out.

Dejected blank faces stared at the ground, refusing to answer.

"I can't believe after one match they deserted the team," Nathan lamented.

His older brother Arie replied, "Nate, it wasn't just a loss, it was a horrifying loss of epic proportions. Our own people stoned us on the way out of town, the Poles taunted us. We didn't score a goal. And we played badly. How can you blame them?"

Of course, few people have the resolve of Nathan. He replaced all the remorse over losing with the joy of knowing the family business was alive and well. He didn't obsess over the bad things. He had a unique ability to see past the present to the desired future.

"He that can't endure the bad, won't live to see the good."

A stranger approached the boys before Nathan could respond to his brother.

"Of course they are down, they were lambs to the slaughter yesterday," intoned Bela Sebesteyn as he strode confidently toward Nathan.

Bela Sebesteyn was forty-five years old, born in 1885 in Hungary. By 1930, he was considered an old man in that day and age. Average life expectancy was just forty years for a man born in the 1800s in these times. Thanks to plagues, poor sanitation, natural disasters, limited medical technology, and war, most men did not live very long by today's standards.

So, Bela was indeed an old man, more than twice Nathan's twenty-one years. But Nathan, being impetuous and supremely confident, plus team captain and head of the Berman family business, would not be bowed by this stranger's bold and sudden advance.

"Who are you and what do you know about soccer?" Nathan shot back at Bela, aiming to make sure his few teammates present still understood he was in charge of this team.

"What you need Sir Captain, is a competent coach. And to your great luck you have just met him: Bela

Sebesteyn is my name and, if you'll forgive the rhyme, soccer is most decidedly my game. I happened to be in Warsaw yesterday and watched you play. Soccer is decidedly not your game yet, but it most definitely can be, with work."

"Ha!" Nathan snorted. "You're a Jew like us, and you're old. How can soccer be your game? We are the first Jewish team ever in this league."

That was all the opening Bela needed. He proceeded into an oration as only an emotionally charged coach with powerful credentials can do.

"I am Bela Sebesteyn, former winger for MTK Budapest, the best soccer team in all of Europe and sometimes, even the world," the soon-to-be coach said, while pausing for effect.

"And I am a Jew."

The boys snapped to attention quickly and fell silent. Could this be true? A Jew, who played winger for the best team in all of Hungary? If it was true, they had just met their first sporting hero.

"What is MTK Budapest? We have never heard of it," Nathan asked in a more controlled voice that began to border on respect.

"I am glad you asked, Sir Captain," Bela said, continuing to give Nathan a respectful nod as the team leader. "MTK Budapest is a local soccer club that also played on the international level. I was a winger. You don't know what a winger is yet, as evidenced by ten of you playing defense yesterday. But you will learn—and soon. This I promise as your new coach."

Nathan had to know with no uncertainty if this man was real or a con artist. He owed it to his team to be sure. "Sir, this may be true. But Hungary is a long way from here. Forgive us if we've never heard of this team..."

"Tell me, have you heard of the Olympic Games?" Sebestyn cut in before Nathan could say more. "Specifically, the 1912 Olympic Games? I played winger on the Hungarian national team. Yes, me a Jew. We beat Austria 3 - 0 in the first round, and I want you to guess who we beat next..."

By now, even Nathan was enraptured. A real soccer player from a high level was here in their midst. And he was a Jew like them. In the Olympics!?!

"Who?!" they all shouted in excited unison.

Bela raised himself up to his full height of five feet six inches and said in a dramatic tone, "We beat Germany, 3 - 1..." and he left the remark hanging so it would take complete dramatic effect.

The boys were, of course, well aware of who the Germans were since they felt their presence profoundly during World War I. The Germans had tanks, planes, and a massive army that stormed over Poland's meager cavalry.

Yet, this man says his team beat the very best the Germans could field in soccer!

The boys exploded in excited questions, rapid fire:

"How did you do this?"

"By learning how to play the game from a good coach."

"Jews were allowed to join this team?"

"Yes, obviously, and I was not the only Jew on the team."

"The Germans?!?!"

"Yes, the Germans and we beat them soundly."

"Budapest is a long way from here, how far?"

"It is some 850 kilometers, but it's much closer than Stockholm...where the Olympic Stadium is located. We played in front of 25,000 cheering spectators."

"What was it like to play in the Olympics?"

"And before you can ask, no, we did not medal. We lost in the second round by a score of 7 - 0, so you see, I know what it feels like to be badly beaten, shut out by a better team," Sebestyn told them. "But that loss was to the eventual gold medal winner, Great Britain, so there was no shame in it."

He had them now in the palm of his hand; even Nathan gave his undivided attention.

"And there is no shame in your loss yesterday, either. I need to speak individually to anyone on this team who feels otherwise," Bela preached and paused for effect.

"The only shame is failing to try. Yesterday, you were overmatched, but you played with heart and never quit. Even if you had played a strong, smart game—which you did not—you might still have been beaten..."

"Every game you play always has the distinct chance

of defeat. If we only enter the games we think we can win without trying, what purpose is there in that? The point of sport is to challenge yourself in the utmost way... Physically, mentally, even spiritually..."

"If you accept my coaching—and I will not be easy—I guarantee you the next time you walk on a soccer pitch, you will feel confident in your abilities, you will know your weaknesses and have a strategy to win in spite of them!"

The boys erupted in cheers. They mobbed Bela. Nathan, though, stood back and waited until he could approach the coach, man to man. The coach's way with words reminded Nathan of his late father, Alter. He, too, could use the power of words to lift you up and make you see what can be, not just what is in front of you.

Alter often said, "He that can't endure the bad will not live to see the good."

Nathan stepped up to Bela. "Sir, as captain of the team, I would like to ask if you would honor us, become our coach and help us become as good as we can be?" Nathan asked with genuine respect.

"Sir Captain," the coach replied with dramatic flourish and a small bow, "I am honored to become coach of Team Premium. Now, I will give you my first instructions."

"First off, get to every member of this team and tell them to meet here for practice tomorrow, late afternoon. No exceptions. Anyone who fails to show up will be left off the team. Good teams demand respect of one another and discipline.

"Second, gather up some more players from nearby towns and convince a Christian or two to join us. All my teams had Jews and Christians on them. We're not a religious endeavor, we want good soccer players regardless. Understand?"

Nathan held up his hand and answered after the coach nodded toward him, allowing him permission to speak.

"Yes, coach, I know a few. We do business with many of the farmers nearby. One family, the Borucs, have sons who might play. I've kicked the ball around with them a few times," Nathan replied. "They're good people and honest business partners. Their father was a good friend to my father. I'll ask him if some of his boys can join us."

"Good!" Bela said with gusto. "Gather everyone together here right on time for practice. Tomorrow, we begin to learn how this game is really played."

NOTE: Bela Sebesteyn was a real person, one of the greatest wingers in Hungarian soccer history. Actual details of his soccer experiences are as described in this story. Since the Kaluszyn soccer program was initiated by the Bund, it is very likely it would have funded just such a coach.

A very small detail about Bela's soccer experience was changed for effect. Hungary actually played Germany first and then Austria. But Hungary did indeed beat them both before losing to Gold Medalist Great Britain.

Bela was known as a quintessential team player with lightning speed and devastating passing skills. He only scored two goals in his international career because he would pass up the opportunity to allow a teammate a scoring chance. He was a very staunch believer in the power of teamwork and would certainly have made that a hallmark of his coaching style.

It is entirely wishful thinking, however, that Bela wound up in Kaluszyn and coached the boys' team. We chose his name to honor Bela's great accomplishments in real life that included a starting role on the 1912 Hungarian Olympic team.

See "Resources" in Appendix for more details on Bela.

CHAPTER EIGHT

PREPARATION, ANTICIPATION, AND COMMUNICATION

Kaluszyn, 1930

AS HE PROMISED TO COACH BELA, NATHAN MADE a trip to the nearby farm of the Boruc family. They were good business partners of the Bermans, supplying many fine sheepskins to the factory over many years.

Most importantly, Mr. Boruc had been good friends with his late father, Alter. Nathan always found them to be honest, and the sons friendly. On many visits, he and the boys would spend some time kicking the ball around and having a bit of fun after business discussions were concluded.

He approached the head of the household, Anatol Boruc, and respectfully asked his permission to invite two of the boys to join the team. The boys overheard this and anxiously took up a position behind their father. Their mother, Jolanta, heard also and she sidled up next to Anatol, whose demeanor was rather stoic and stern compared to her infectious ebullience. This was a big thing. Farm families like the Borucs did not often leave the farm, except for weddings and funerals. The idea that two of the boys would regularly go to Kaluszyn for practice and places like Warsaw for games—well, that was a big thing to consider.

Anatol engaged Nathan in a lengthy conversation on all the specific details. Not unlike one of their business negotiations, the back and forth continued for some time. Anatol was not warm to the idea, but fortunately for Nathan, Jolanta made her positive opinion known in subtle, but powerful ways. Occasionally she would make a brief comment, like, "Oh Warsaw, the boys should see how the produce market works there."

The boys held their tongues, but it was obvious they desperately wanted the chance to play for the team.

Nathan had exhausted every argument he could think of, when finally, Anatol suddenly said, "tak," which simply means "yes" in Polish. The boys let out a loud whoop, unable to contain their excitement. Jolanta smiled and nodded her approval.

"However," Anatol interjected forcefully, "there will be no missing of chores tolerated. Not once! Is this understood? Your jobs on this farm come before kicking a ball around."

Nathan shook Anatol's hand and said, "Done. We will make sure soccer does not interfere with work. That's necessary and true for all of us on this team."

That night, for the first time in a while, Nathan slept like a rock. The next day, he would present the Boruc boys to Coach Bela. And the team would begin anew with a real coach guiding them.

Back in Kaluszyn, word about the coach had quickly spread among the team. A real Olympic player was going to teach them? A Jew? All of the boys eagerly showed up for practice the next day, including the two newcomers.

"Coach," Nathan said as he stood alongside the Borucs, "I want to introduce you to our newest players. Stanislaw Boruc, who is twenty-one like me, and his younger brother, Teobold, who is eighteen."

Coach Bela was pleased. Two strapping young Poles would be a good addition, even if they could not play expertly. At the least, it would show other teams that Team Premium was not restricted to Jews alone and it might diminish the cruel catcalls that disheartened his boys and threw them off their games.

"Welcome, Borucs! I am very pleased to meet you," Coach Bela said. "Now, everyone come introduce yourselves to our newest members. We are Team Premium and we stand as one against our opponents!"

The boys greeted one another and chattered excitedly until Coach blew his whistle, signaling the start of practice.

Coach Bela began teaching the boys the fundamentals of the game. Prior to his arrival, practices amounted to little more than playground antics with the boys taking endless shots at the goal. Every boy ran to the ball at once, wanting to kick it toward the goal.

That ended today. Coach Bela began by running the boys through very basic drills—how to dribble the ball, how to trap it when receiving a pass or stealing one, passing the ball to a teammate, tackling to steal the ball—the basic aspects of handling the ball outside of shooting it toward the goal.

The boys, of course, did not understand where the coach was going with all of this. "How can we win if we never shoot the ball?"

Coach Bela called the team together.

"All right, I am now going to reveal to you how we beat the Austrians and the Germans," he said. "Both of these teams had big, strong, fast athletes who were among the best in the entire world. Our team, on the other hand, was not the biggest or the fastest. So how did we win?"

The team was dumbfounded by the question. How indeed?

"We played smarter. We were mentally faster than our opponents," Coach Bela answered for them. "And now, Team Premium is going to train to play smart and mentally fast."

Coach Bela showed them techniques that would allow them to overcome their relative lack of experience, speed, and power. The game strategy was focused on zone defense and taking the offensive opportunities created by it.

Anticipate:

As the attacking midfielder prepares to pass the ball, watch his eyes and take off running immediately to that space. Don't overthink and wait for the ball to be kicked—just go! This is a game like chess; think a move ahead. Follow the attacker's eyes and anticipate, move into that passing lane, and intercept the ball. Simply running after it has been kicked is playing checkers. Play chess. Don't react. Anticipate.

Engage:

Get to the attacker quickly, close up the space between you. Don't run straight, approach him on an angle. Stay low to the ground, on the balls of your feet to keep your balance. Never lunge at the ball, instead try to force him backward. When he is close, keep an outstretched arm on him and when you turn to chase the ball, push off him. Be physical, give a little push! When appropriate, don't be afraid to execute a tackle.

Communicate:

Without good communication, team defense is impossible. There will be a breakdown and the opposing team will capitalize. Talk to one another constantly. For example, the first defender to reach the ball should yell, "I have pressure," the second should move in behind him and favor one side and yell, "I have cover on the left."

And so, the first defender now knows he should force the attacker to the left toward a trap with his teammate. The best soccer teams in the world constantly talk to one another. They learn to think and move as one.

There were many more drills taught by Coach Bela. But he purposefully tried to keep things simple and direct so the boys, so raw in their abilities, could absorb it and learn. And most importantly, so they could feel what it's like to master each skill and in so doing, build their confidence more and more each time.

In their very next game, Coach was pleased to find he had a natural scorer in Stanislaw Boruc. While he only managed a couple of goals over the next several games, they were solid goals and they helped boost the entire team's confidence.

Most importantly, Coach saw that the team was gradually shaping into one, solid, chess-playing unit. They were communicating with each other. And while they did not always execute physically, they were jelling mentally. It gave him great pleasure to witness the transformation.

As you teach, you learn.

Coach Bela hadn't felt like this since his playing days. He looked forward to each day with great anticipation. Who would step up today and enjoy the triumph of having mastered something new?

And then suddenly, a tragic turn of events threatened to derail the team.

Stanislaw's father, Anatol, suddenly pulled his boys

from the team. Chores on the farm fell behind by a full day, partly due to soccer practice and partly to Stanislaw and Teobold getting caught up in youthful hijinks with Nathan after practice.

The details are not important. But missing a day's worth of chores was a critical misstep on a farm. It was the single prohibition placed by Anatol on his sons' involvement with the team. And they broke it.

Nathan was beside himself. For a few hours of mindless pleasure, he had cost his team its goal scorer and cost the Boruc boys the joys of being on the team. There was nothing he could do to turn back the clock. And little to anything he could ever say to Anatol, the stern taskmaster, to make up for the lost time.

It was a "katastrofe" of epic proportion. It was bad enough that his actions cost the team, which still had to face the tough squad from Warsaw in a rematch at the close of the season. But now, he had also perhaps damaged a business partnership with a man who had been his father's good friend, as well as curtailing the developing friendship between himself and the Boruc boys.

Nathan's head and heart ached. So many thoughts caromed in his mind. As he often did in times of great stress, he returned to the comforting words of his father, Alter, who seemed to always know what to say to reset a scene.

Alter often said, "He that can't endure the bad, will not live to see the good."

But how would enduring this fix anything? Nathan pondered. Almost in direct reply, another favorite saying of his father's came to him. "Ton nit klug in verter zeyn klug in meshim."

"Do not be wise in words, be wise in deeds."

"Of course!" Nathan said aloud to himself. "It may not fix everything, but it will be a worthwhile attempt."

Nathan ran breathlessly to the home where Coach Bela was staying. The coach had been recruited by the Bund to run its new sports program. There were very few accomplished Jewish athletes in Poland. But Budapest was a relative treasure trove of Jewish athletic talent. The town was very fortunate to acquire the services of such an accomplished coach.

Nathan breathlessly laid out his plan to Coach Bela. Nathan was very concerned the coach would nullify it. After all, it required that the entire team miss a day's practice. But to his surprise, the coach nodded and gave his approval.

He instructed Nathan, "Just promise me, as captain, you will ensure they communicate and work together as one."

"I promise Coach," Nathan replied and then went about visiting the home of each player to tell them of the plan. They would all meet tomorrow at the appointed time at the farm of Anatol Boruc.

The next day, the entire team gathered at the Borucs' where they found Stanislaw and Teobold hard at work, harvesting in a potato field.

"Everyone grab a basket and follow Stan and Teo's lead. We will harvest this entire section as a team," Nathan directed the boys.

The Boruc boys smiled broadly, grateful for the help, but a bit bewildered. Stan looked at Nate and said, "Are you crazy?"

"Maybe," Nate replied. "We can't go back in time, but we can multiply your efforts here today and give our labor to your father. It's the least we owe."

"Communicate!" Nathan hollered to all the boys. Stanislaw and Teobold gave the team directions on what to pick and how. Other boys took up the slack and passed the information forward to boys further from the group. They talked constantly to one another, just like they did on the soccer field.

Jolanta Boruc, the boys' mother, saw the commotion from the farmhouse. After the boys had been working for a few hours, she drew two large buckets of cold sweet water from the deep well and walked them out to the boys. They drank most of it, splashed some on their faces. They showered Mrs. Boruc with gratitude.

"Tell me, boys, is it your habit to descend on farms and take to working the chores?" she laughed. "You're doing a fine job. At this pace, you will have four days' labor accomplished in just one day."

Mrs. Boruc returned to the farmhouse. But came out again two more times; one time, to bring some bread and another time to bring more water. Her thoughtfulness almost made the labor seem easy. The Borucs were strong in their faith in God and placed a high value on honesty and integrity. To her, the boys' actions were an expression of genuine remorse and an effort to make things right. She was very pleased by all of this.

Mr. Boruc never appeared. Mrs. Boruc said he was busy in other fields. Nathan had prepared several points to use in negotiation with Mr. Boruc in an attempt to win forgiveness and permission for the boys to return to the team.

But, he never got the chance, which may have been for the best since Boruc was a man of few words and not one to barter. It was time for the boys to return to Kaluszyn, before sunset. Even though he would not get the chance to talk to Mr. Boruc, Nathan felt they had done the right thing.

Boruc was an honest man. Surely, he would see that they had more than repaid the lost time in the fields. He may not allow his boys to return, but he might at least call it even in terms of Berman business. Nathan hoped most of all that he and Stanislaw could remain good friends.

Another of Alter's oft-repeated expressions popped into Nathan's head:

"Ehren is fil tei'erer far gelt!"

"Honor is dearer than money!"

Both Borucs were present at practice the next day, much to everyone's delight, especially Nathan and Coach Bela.

"Our father said you overpaid your debt and moved the harvest schedule ahead several days, so we are able to return as long as we never miss chores again," Stan announced to the team, which let out a great cheer in reply.

Coach Bela was filled with pride. He had never anticipated how rewarding this coaching assignment could be. His boys were becoming a real team. They were gaining the confidence that comes with mastery of new skills. They were working together as one on the playing field—and even in the potato fields. Such bonding exercises are what makes good teams great.

Soon, they would play the final game of the season, the big rematch with mighty Team Mazzovia of Warsaw. That team had grown even more powerful since the crushing defeat they delivered to Team Premium in the first game. They were presently undefeated and drawing large crowds to their games. Team Premium had yet to win a match, even though they were competitive and came within a goal on several occasions.

As a result of their developing success and mastery of basic game skills, they began to slowly win some in the town over. They actually had a few followers who came out to watch their games.

Coach Bela brought a certain cachet to the team, and a reason for skeptical adults to take notice. "We are coached by an Olympian," they would say, "a Jewish Olympian."

The fact that they said "we" was a real sign of acceptance.

This match would be the greatest challenge yet. Coach Bela's boys had made remarkable progress. They were still a bit behind more experienced teams, but they were learning to think smart and play as one. With every improvement, confidence was gained. Earned. Most importantly, they tightly bonded as brothers and would not quit a fight.

This time, none of them were afraid.

Perhaps, Team Premium would surprise the boys from Warsaw.

Perhaps.

CHAPTER NINE

A WEDDING AND A
SAD TURN OF EVENTS

Kaluszyn, 1930

IT WAS NOW LATE IN AUGUST AND THE BIG rematch in Warsaw was just a week away.

August, or Sierpień in Polish, was a most fortuitous time.

For one thing, much of the harvest had been completed on the local farms.

Nathan and the boys from Team Premium pitched in a few more times at the Borucs, which helped speed things along and earned them the deep gratitude and affection of the Boruc family.

But more importantly, the month of Sierpień had the letter "R" in it and that made it a lucky month. The Polish Catholics had many traditions and superstitions. Lucky months were critical times because these were the only times when Poles would marry.

And there are few events as festive as a Polish wedding, to this Nathan could enthusiastically attest. Poles and Jews mingled together quite often when it came to major social occasions.

The shtetl was not a restricted ghetto in these days. Jews could travel freely as Nathan often did on business. It was not uncommon for a Jew to have friendly ongoing relationships with local farm families. This was the case with the Bermans and the Borucs, as well as the Kaczoreks, Nowaks, and other farmers nearby Kaluszyn.

Many were good business partners, supplying the Bermans with quality sheepskins at fair prices. Nathan was especially friendly with the Boruc and Kaczorek families.

Poles and Jews shared some wedding customs, such as a procession to celebrate the wedding. Very often, Jews performed as musicians at Polish wedding receptions. And as was the case this day, Jews were often among the honored guests along with virtually the entire countryside.

This was the wedding of Nathan's friend Kacper (Casper) Kaczorek and his betrothed Lena Mazur. Once they returned to the Kaczorek farm from the church, the reception would begin in earnest.

"Sto lat," Nathan sang in Polish, along with everyone, as the happy couple arrived. "Sto lat, sto lat, Niech żyje, żyje nam!" The song wishes the couple:

"Good luck, good cheer, may you live a hundred years."

Nathan was most impressed with the intensity and sheer endurance of the participants at a Polish wedding party. Prodigious amounts of vodka would be consumed with even larger amounts of food. The festivities would last all of two or three straight days or even more.

The couple arrived and the reception began in earnest. They were showered with rice as they entered and then their parents presented them with specially baked bread and salt. The bread represented a desire to see the couple prosper and the salt was a reminder to them that life can be bitter at times. Then each was presented with a glass filled with clear liquid. One glass was filled with water, the other with vodka.

This was always a big moment at a Polish wedding that Nathan loved to see unfold. Tradition said whomever received the vodka would be the dominant spouse in the marriage. While formal tradition among Jews and Poles alike defaults to patriarchal dominance, in reality, wives and mothers held sway in the household.

Nathan often mused that this is the real reason why the Bermans held a strict rule against talking about business outside of the factory. After all, if the men discussed business at home, the wives would naturally express their opinions and then who knows where all this might go back inside the factory?

"Tsuris!"

Nathan startled himself by saying the Yiddish word for trouble aloud. He hoped no one noticed.

In a Jewish household, the wife is "akeret habayit," which means the "mainstay" of the household. It is she who largely determines the ways of the home. As far as Nathan could tell, it was exactly the same in a Polish household if not more so. The Poles have a tongue-in-cheek expression that captures it:

"The woman cries before the wedding and the man after."

Nathan and all the guests burst out laughing and cheered as it became obvious that Lena had received the glass with the vodka. The couple drank and then tossed their glasses in the air and as the glasses broke on the floor, everyone shouted, "Gorzko, gorzko!" The words literally mean "bitter, bitter" and are intended to make the newlyweds kiss.

Why bitter? Because only a kiss between the bride and groom can sweeten the mood of the guests: their kiss takes away the bitterness, and of course another shot of vodka all around helps, too. Often the guests are not satisfied with the first kiss and demand another, followed by another round of vodka. And on it goes.

Polish and Jewish customs meshed well together. Everyone cheered as the small band, made up of mostly Jewish musicians from Kaluszyn, struck up the Jewish folk song "Hava Nagila." It was, after all, a very catchy tune that is fun and easy to dance to regardless of your religion.

Nathan was familiar with a new Jewish folk dance that originated in the Balkans just a couple years earlier. It is credited to the famous choreographer and dancer, Baruch Agadati, who would later immigrate to Israel.

The dance is called the Hora, a circle dance. Nathan had attended a Jewish wedding in Warsaw last year where they added a new twist to this dance that everyone really enjoyed.

Emboldened by several shots of vodka, Nathan rushed up to his friend Casper and bride Lena and excitedly explained his idea for the Hora dance. The bride and groom seemed to love it as they laughed and slapped Nathan on the back. Casper motioned for all his younger friends to come join them on the dance floor. After some quick instructions to some of the groomsmen, the dance began.

This time, the stronger young men like Stanislaw hoisted Casper up on a chair. Others lifted Lena on a chair of her own. As the others circled around them, the chairs danced in midair as the band again played *Hava Nagila*.

Fortunately, after a few close calls, neither the bride nor groom were dropped from their chairs. Everyone in the wedding party enjoyed the new dance immensely. And of course, as soon as the newlyweds' feet touched the ground, the chants began: "Gorzko! Gorzko!"

Later on at midnight, the bridal veil would be removed and her long braid cut and unbraided in a ceremony called "oczepiny," which will symbolize Lena's transition from girlhood into a married woman.

For now, more games. Not surprisingly, they involved more drinking and more dancing. Throughout the night and the days ahead, the crowd will chant "Gorzko!!!"

again and again. If they are not pleased with the kiss that results, they will demand a better kiss by singing songs. They will refuse to drink again until a satisfactory kiss is made. So, there is nonstop singing, kissing, and drinking for several days.

Polish wedding parties are very much a group activity. This was Nathan's kind of party. There was no arguing or anger. Just joy, singing, and celebration and lots of food and vodka.

Later, he and Stanislaw, Sam, Chaim, Teobold, and some other boys would sneak out and kick the soccer ball around. They would all have to leave the party soon to get home before sunset, which fortunately happens very late on an August night in the country.

Tomorrow, there would be practice with Coach Bela. In a week's time, they would be on the road to Warsaw to face the mighty Team Mazzovia again. Their level of confidence was at its highest since the coach first took over.

The boys dreamed about this upcoming game. In their hearts, they knew they would win. They believed in each other and in their team.

For the moment, though, life was just too good and easy in the gentle countryside of Kaluszyn. Of course, a hangover would greet them in the morning. But for right now, this was a time for laughter, fellowship, fun, and, of course, more vodka.

Life in this moment in time could not be better.

* * *

"Nathan, wake up!" sister Fay called out, shaking Nathan awake. "Doctor Silver is at Symcha's house. Lybel's bout with typhus has taken a turn for the worse."

Nathan dressed quickly and ran to his brother's house. Doctor Silver greeted him. "Our only hope to save Lybel is with an antibiotic, doxycycline. Frimers in Warsaw is the nearest dispensary."

"It's Shabbos!" someone wailed. "No trucks are traveling to Warsaw."

Typical of his problem-solving bravado, Nathan responded before he could even come up with a plan. "Don't worry, I'll be back within the day with the drugs."

Nathan ran to Frank's house and explained the situation. Frank's family owned a trucking and transportation company. Within a few short minutes, they were in a truck and on their way to Warsaw.

The streets of Kaluszyn were empty as most people were either home or in Shul in observance of the Shabbos. Warsaw would be different. Most residents of Warsaw were gentiles. The streets would be crowded with families going about their Saturday business.

Frank gunned the truck as fast as it would go down the long and bumpy road to Warsaw. Nathan knew the Warsaw streets well, since the family maintained a retail shop there. As they reached the city, he directed Frank through a shortcut to Frimers, and the two ran inside almost before the truck was stopped.

Nathan quickly explained their urgent need and was back in the truck within minutes, drugs in hand. The distance back to Kaluszyn was slightly more than thirty-six miles, but on this dirt road in an old truck, it took several hours.

Frank pushed the truck to full speed the whole teeth-jarring way. He would apologize later to his father if they bent the frame on a particularly jolting bump in the road. This was life or death. The truck could be repaired. But Lybel...

Little Lybel Schmiel was only five years old. The thought of losing such a precious little member of the family was unacceptable. If only they could fly.

Back at Symcha's, Nathan leapt from the moving truck as Frank slammed on the brakes. They burst through the door praying they were in time to save Lybel.

But they were greeted by tears.

Lybel had passed away some fifteen minutes before they arrived. It's doubtful that even the antibiotics could have saved him that day.

All Nathan and Frank could do was console Symcha and his wife, Ethel, as best they could. Sobbing and tears overwhelmed any words they might have spoken. There would be time for prayers later. For now, they simply held each other as tightly as they could.

CHAPTER TEN

THE FINAL REMATCH

Warsaw, 1930

THE MOOD IN KALUSZYN TOWARD ITS SOCCER team had changed dramatically over the course of the season. While Team Premium did not rack up any big victories, it did record goals and played with increasing competence. They were an up-and-coming team deserving of respect. And Coach Bela's reputation and presence in the community made a real impact.

In the meantime, the Haskalah movement had loosened tensions between the strictly conservative religious and those with a more liberal view. Those events combined factors to make possible the small, but enthusiastic group of followers who regularly watched the team play. As many as a dozen townsfolk planned to make the trip to Warsaw to see the big rematch. Of course, they might also visit the markets while there, as well. That would serve the team well, since Team Mazzovia's ongoing winning streak had built quite a following in Warsaw. For certain, their side of the field would be two or three deep with hundreds of vocal followers.

Coach Bela was purposefully subdued on the ride to the playing pitch. He let the boys release pent-up energy with their typical banter and boasts. That was fine for now, to burn off nervous tension. He would quiet them before they approached the field.

The transports rolled to a stop a short distance from the pitch. After the boys disembarked, Coach Bela called them together, along with the dozen townsfolk who came to support them, and began his address. Bela had heard and given many pregame talks before. The best talks, he knew, were short and focused on a common foe they could rally against as one. In this instance, it was not especially hard to conjure up the demon they faced.

"You boys have worked very hard, and no matter what happens today, I will always be very proud of you. Most of the time, I have told you it does not matter if we win or lose. Today? Today is different."

"This is the last game of our season. Some of you will choose not to play next season. Our team will never be exactly the same again. In a certain sense, this is our final game together."

"I was there the last time you played Team Mazzovia here on this field. I remember the catcalls, the jeers, and the insults you endured," he said, and paused for effect. "I also remember how badly we played that day," he said with a wink, drawing nervous laughter from his charges. "But that was a hundred years ago compared to how you play today." He raised his voice for effect. "You are a different team now, a real team. And you've spent the past many weeks becoming a smart team that plays as one."

The boys cheered in response. Coach Bela shifted into a higher gear. "This crowd may again get ugly. Even our Polish players may suffer abuse because city folk often look down on farmers. They call them backward bumpkins."

"No, they are not!" Sam and Nathan shouted in unison.

"You're right! Our farmers are our brothers and great members of our team."

"Yes they are!" all the Jewish boys answered.

"And I don't have to remind you how some people here treat Jewish people. Expect to hear all of that again—but do not let it distract you!"

"They will not!" Stanislaw's deep, impassioned baritone led all the boys in reply.

"Most games, I coached you to improve as players and as a team. I really did not focus on winning. Today, though, I am coaching you to win. Are you ready to slay these giants?"

"We are READY!!!" the team shouted as one.

It was important the boys believed that their coach truly believed they could win. Deep down, Bela did indeed believe they would.

While they were still huddled together, Stan raised

his hand and requested to speak. This surprised everyone. Stan was much like his father, silent and downright stoic most of the time. But when he spoke, people paid attention because it was such a rare occurrence.

"Yes, Stanislaw," Coach Bela said. "What is on your mind?"

"There is nothing any of these city people can say that will deter us," Stan said with a slight emotional tremble in his deep voice. "We are brothers. Not just myself and Teo—all of us are brothers. We are Team Premium, and we cannot be broken!"

Everyone, including the Kaluszyn townsfolk, let out a loud "Hurrah!" Nathan, swept up by the powerful emotions, hollered at the top of his lungs,

"Rak?"

"Can we be this?"

All assembled, gathered close and answered, "Chazak Amats!"

"Be strong, stand firm with courage, and fear not!"

On the other side of the pitch, Team Mazzovia entered as they had before, as if they were executing a military drill. As they crisply encircled their half of the field, they chanted their battle cry, "Na Wroga!" meaning "On the enemy!" in Polish.

Team Premium ignored them and concentrated instead on their warm-up drills. They were hyperfocused and ready for this rematch. As the referees signaled the game was about to begin, the team huddled together again.

"I want you to use this mind trick," Coach Bela told the boys as they gathered on the sideline. "Every time you hear a vile remark, associate it with the sound one of the Borucs' hogs make when it has a bad case of flatulence. Every vile remark is just a burst of gas from a hole in the back of a hog."

The boys roared in laughter. This was good. He wanted them to loosen up and be prepared to deal with the hatred and cheap shots, to let them bounce off. It was a good distraction and it worked. Laughter is a strong shield.

Coach Bela had spent the past few weeks drilling the team on a new formation. It was one designed to help a smaller, slower opponent contend with superior physical talent.

He guided them into a 5-4-1 formation, putting his best players in the fewer key offensive positions, and his best communicators as the larger group of defenders.

Stanislaw Boruc in the 1 position was the team's lone striker, positioned directly in front of the opposition's goalkeeper. Behind Stan, Nate filled the role of attacking midfielder. Positioned closer to the midfield line were a pair of wingers on left and right sides. Sam took the left side and Teobold Boruc took the right. Behind them at midfield, was Arie, a center midfielder. These were the main attackers, relying heavily on the skills of the single striker.

Defense was the primary focus. It was made up of three defenders tightly positioned ahead of the goalkeeper. They were never to leave the defensive zone.

On each side of them was a winger whose first priority was to pinch in on defense. But they were allowed to travel into the offensive zone just past midfield to support an attack.

The principal aim of Bela's strategy was to keep the score low, frustrate the fast-running Warsaw team and get lucky on occasion on offense. "There is nothing wrong with being opportunistic and taking advantage of an odd bounce," he reminded himself often.

As always, he stressed the fundamentals:

- Anticipate: Read their eyes. Get to the space before the ball is kicked.
- Engage: Be physical. Close up the space between you and the attacker.
- Communicate: Talk constantly. Alert one another of dangers and opportunities.

The catcalls rang out as the referees called the teams to begin the match. Coach Bela took his own advice and ignored them. He said a little prayer to himself, portions of Psalm 35 as best he remembered it: *"Let those who seek to kill me be disgraced and humiliated. Let those who plan to harm me be turned back and ashamed. Let them be like chaff in the wind, with the angel of the Lord driving them away. Let their way be dark and slippery, with the angel of the Lord pursuing them."*

Bela chuckled as he finished because he recalled a similar prayer an Irishman taught him over drinks at a Stockholm tavern during the Olympics:

"May those who love us, love us. And for those who don't, may God turn their hearts. And if he can't turn their hearts, may he twist their ankles so that we can know them by their limping. Amen."

The game began.

Team Mazzovia scored a quick goal due to a lapse in the defense that Coach Bela ascribed to nervousness. This judgment seemed to be correct, since Team Premium played brilliantly for the rest of the half, holding the mighty, undefeated Warsaw team to just that single goal.

The score was 1 – 0 at the intermission.

Bela did not waste time and emotion on another speech. He could tell his boys were enthused and confident. He kept their focus on reviews of select plays and what could be improved next time. That was all he could do at this point—coach them. The game was in the boys' hands.

The match resumed.

As often happens with a bigger, stronger opponent, Team Mazzovia wore the boys down and added to its score in the second half, taking a 2 – 0 lead into the final five minutes of play. Since there are no time-outs in soccer, Coach Bela used the hand signals he had taught his captain, Nathan, to adjust the game strategy.

Nathan caught the coach's signals and barked out orders to his teammates. They would go more on the attack now, bringing the wingers up further into the offensive zone closer to the midfield wingers, who in turn crowded closer to the opposing goal.

The move created two decent opportunities almost immediately, but the opposing defense was strong and turned them away. Nathan and the rest of the boys kept their focus and continued supporting one another. Communicating.

Suddenly, a bit of luck, an odd bounce, and Sam found himself with the ball on the left wing. He trapped it, took a deep breath, and dribbled toward midfield. Nathan, the attacking midfielder, was behind Stan, the striker. A defender was closing in behind Stan's right side.

Nathan called out to Stan, "On your right!"

Stan moved to more open space on the left, where Sam saw him and drilled a pass. Stan trapped it and, realizing he did not have a clear shot, passed it back to Nathan who had moved to open space on the left side of the goalkeeper. Nathan let it fly as soon as it reached him and sent the ball zipping toward the goal, just above the keeper's head.

And it clanged hard against the crossbar, then bounced quickly back onto the field. It took a funny turn and came straight into Stan, who wound up and fired it back like a rocket to the right side of the keeper and...

"GOOOOOOAAAL!!!"

Team Premium shouted as one. Their townsfolk standing on the sideline, Coach Bela and every player erupted as if they had just won Olympic gold.

"GOOOOALLLL!!!!"

Stan, Teo, Sam, Arie, and Nate hugged on the field. Everyone tried to quickly regain their composure to avoid a penalty with the referees. There were still a few minutes to play, still a great chance to win.

Both teams buckled down on defense. There were no clear chances for either side as time ran out.

The score held: 2 – 1 for Team Mazzovia.

But it could just as easily have been a win as far as Coach Bela was concerned. He gathered his boys together on the sideline, along with their jubilant supporters, who, while not expert in understanding soccer, knew their boys had just acquitted themselves quite well against the best of the best in the Polish Premier League.

"I'm sorry we lost, Coach, if we only had more time," Nathan said, sincere in his disappointment.

"But you did win today," Coach Bela replied.

"Maybe not in the final score, but in the way you played. With heart. With smart communication. Like a band of brothers. As a real team."

"We held them to many fewer goals this time," Sam chimed in.

"And you did much more than that," the coach answered. "Listen! Tell me what do you hear? I'll answer for you: it's SILENCE. No more catcalls and jeers like before. You have earned something that is more valuable than a trophy. You have earned RESPECT."

Everyone on the sideline was kvelling. The assembled townsfolk cheered, "Yasher koach! May you have the strength to continue doing so well."

Back in Kaluszyn they were greeted with applause and admiration. The boys were shocked by the outpouring of respect and honor. No more stones!

One of the boys loudly exclaimed, "It's as if we are rabbis! What a wonderful feeling!"

Rabbi Avraham Gombiner was in earshot and heard the young man. The boy's comment made him smile as he thought to himself, "Nu? If only I got such an enthusiastic and joyful greeting every time I returned to town. I should be so lucky."

He stopped the boys as they were about to disembark the transport. "Young men, you should take a very important lesson from this day."

The boys held back their chatter and listened with respect. It sounded as if a lecture was coming, but they knew better than to disrespect a rabbi. Teaching important lessons is, after all, what rabbis do.

"The Torah does not define the righteous as someone who has won a battle or even as someone who has amassed great material success," he said, drawing the boys' interest. "The Torah tells us the righteous is someone who has persevered. It is written in King Solomon, Proverbs, 24:16: 'A righteous man falls down seven times... and gets up.'

These people are not cheering because you almost won a soccer game," he concluded. "They cheer because you refused to lie down."

CHAPTER ELEVEN

AUTOBIOGRAPHY OF A SURVIVOR, PART III

Kaluszyn, 1933–Joseph Berman

IN 1933, HITLER AND HIS NAZI PARTY CAME TO power in neighboring Germany. An anti-Jewish campaign was sweeping through Germany, which also affected Eastern Europe. In Poland, the parliament passed anti-Jewish laws, which made it legal to preach that gentiles should not buy things from Jewish merchants or products manufactured by Jewish companies.

But in our city of Kaluszyn, 80 percent of the population was Jewish, and things were not so bad. Life continued as usual, but the economic situation for Jews began to deteriorate. I remember there was a rule that our company had to take in a gentile in order to be able to bid on government contracts, and his name had to appear as the main contractor. Of course, we had to pay well for that, and it made us less competitive, as most of our competitors were gentile firms.

That forced us to turn to the retail business. We opened a wholesale and retail store in Warsaw, and also rented an apartment there. The store was very successful, and we were doing well.

It was 1936, and I was nineteen years old. Hitler devoted all his efforts to rearming Germany, in preparation for war. I was called for a physical by the Polish army, which I passed with a Grade A. I was not called into service until March 1938, however. I was first stationed in a city called Lomza, about 180 kilometers from home. It was about twenty kilometers from the eastern part of Prussia (Germany).

My first three months in the service were very hard, and you had to do your best to prove yourself. Because of my excellent record in target shooting, I was assigned to a special group of about sixty soldiers called the Sharpshooters Group. I was the only Jew in the group, but I did not have much difficulty with the anti-Semitism of the gentile boys, because after a short time they realized that I could do everything better than they could.

I also became the secretary to our lieutenant and spent much time doing office work, but each morning till noon, I had to take part in all exercises. I also joined the soccer team for our regiment. That gave me three times a week away from army duties, to train with the soccer team.

On one occasion, I was summoned by the officer in charge of the prison. He had been informed that I knew my way around Warsaw, and told me that they had a prisoner who had received a life sentence for killing two people. He had to be taken to the capital and delivered to the prison there.

I was chosen to transport him. I could not very well refuse. Besides, this gave me a chance to visit my brother Nathan, my sister Chaya, and her husband. They were taking care of the store in Warsaw. It was late fall 1938.

I had to get up at 2:00 a.m. to report to the prison. When I arrived, they gave me all of the prisoner's records, which were to be handed over to the officer in charge of the prison in Warsaw. It was a very dark night, and there was a mixture of rain and snow falling.

I had to walk to the train station, which was more than two kilometers away from the base prison barracks. The prisoner turned out to be someone I knew from the first weeks in the army. I loaded my rifle in front of him, and released the safety. I told him not to try anything stupid or I would have to shoot him.

When we got to the station, the railroad servicemen already knew about us. They gave us a separate cabin on the train. It took about four hours to get to Warsaw. When we arrived, I hired a horse and buggy and delivered the criminal to the prison. I was free after that, and was given an extra day to spend in Warsaw.

CHAPTER TWELVE

THE PROPOSAL

Kaluszyn, 1938

THE SUN BEGAN TO SET ON THE AUTUMN DAY. Jozefa Pitsudskieso Street was bustling. Yiddish and Polish could be heard as the many merchants prepared their goods for the long trek to the Warsaw market. Many of the men were Hasidic Jews, sporting long beards, and wearing long black coats and hats. The woman were dressed modestly in long dresses that covered their legs and arms.

Farther down the street stood Natalia Rudzinka's restaurant. The jukebox was playing the latest recordings from Warsaw. The tango was the latest craze and Janusz Poplawski was Poland's favorite artist. Nathan, Sam, and Frank were seated at their regular table. A bottle of vodka, fresh kielbasa, and pierogi made their way around the table.

"Nathan," Frank called out, "I have a truck headed

to Warsaw tomorrow morning if that would work out for you."

"Perfect," said Nathan. "That will get me in town a day before the hides are due to arrive from the Baltic, and I will have time to visit with Nechema and her family."

"Vay is mier," cried out Sam. "Does this mean what I think?"

"Yes," said Nathan. "I will see her father, and ask for his daughter's hand in marriage. Pour another round and wish me luck. Raise your glasses, my family. La chaim—to life."

The next morning, Nathan traveled to Warsaw, where he would knock on the Bernsteins' door and announce his desire to marry Nechema. Her parents would not be surprised. After all, they liked Nathan very much. He was the leader of the well-known Berman family. He ran the factory in Kaluszyn and the retail store there in Warsaw. He was a prize catch!

Nathan would fit right in with the crowds around him in Warsaw. He put on his best (and only) double-breasted suit and topped it off with a fedora. He enjoyed the liveliness of Miodawa Street as he walked.

He skipped up the steps of the Bernstein home and knocked three times. The door swung open and ten-year-old Shlomo emerged, jumping into Nathan's arms with squeals of happiness. What better greeting is there than the joy and uncompromising love of a child?

"So happy you're here, Nathan! I missed you! Please

come in," Mrs. Bernstein greeted him. The smell of chulent and challa filled the room as she approached with her babushka and apron on. "So happy you'll be joining us for the Shabbos."

"My pleasure, and so nice to see you," Nathan said, and handed her the fresh flowers he purchased on his walk over.

In future visits, Nathan would be presented with chosenbrod, a traditional pastry presented, even to this day in Poland, to the betrothed upon a visit. It was the day he would first make his proposal.

"The flowers are beautiful! Thank you, Nathan. Mr. Bernstein is in the study. Why don't you go say hello?"

Nathan walked down the hall and presented himself to his beloved's father for approval. As a preliminary in their conversation, Mr. Bernstein first required a report on Nathan's lot in life and ability to care for his daughter.

"All is well!" Nathan responded. "The store here is very profitable. And the factory in Kaluszyn is very busy. We have received new orders for sheepskins from the railroad and the military. The military orders doubled this year."

"I'm not surprised," said Mr. Bernstein. "There's a big concern that Hitler will make a move on our sovereignty. Glad to hear the Polish government is stepping up to meet the threat."

Nathan bit his lip rather than respond to that remark. "The Germans have tanks and planes while we have horses," Nathan thought to himself. "It would take a miracle if it comes to us against them, but let's not preoccupy our minds with another possible war."

Instead of engaging in debate, he began the age-old ritual. "Mr. Bernstein, you know how fond I am of your daughter. I believe we can have a future together. I ask for your blessings and permission to seek her hand in marriage."

"Of course, Nathan," an ebullient Mr. Bernstein said. "Congratulations! You're one of the finest young gentlemen I have ever met. Let us drink to the future. La chaim!"

As the sun began to set, the family gathered around the table. Candles were lit, the bread was cut, and the wine was poured. Nathan rose from his seat, standing to the side of Nechema. He lowered to one knee and took her hand. "Since I first set eyes upon you, my thoughts and hopes were that one day you would become my wife. I promise to do everything in my power to make you the happiest woman in Poland."

"Will you please take me to be your husband and from the two we shall become one?"

Nachema broke down as tears flowed from her eyes. "Yes, of course, Nathan, I will marry you."

Mr. Bernstein gave a toast. "Now it is time to drink! Raise your glasses to the future Mr. and Mrs. Nathan Berman! To life!"

Joy and happiness surrounded the Shabbos dinner. There would be time later to draft the Ketubah, a special type of Jewish prenuptial agreement that is an integral part of the Kiddushin (betrothal) process. The Ketubah would spell out all of the rights and responsibilities of the groom in relation to the bride.

But this moment was about celebration, not details.

After Shabbos, Nathan said his farewells, gave Schlomo a bear hug and then headed for his nearby storefront. Once there, Nathan bounded up the stairs to a small bedroom and immediately drifted off to sleep. Tomorrow, he would return to Kaluszyn. For now, sleep. Finally, sleep.

The next morning, at the Warsaw hide market, Nate was happy to see the stacks of sheepskin tagged for the Bermans' factory back in Kaluszyn. His trips through Europe had paid off; he was able to obtain high-quality sheepskin at a fair market price.

The best hides in Europe were secured for the factory, and there were many. His love agreed to marry him. One day, he and Nechema would have a child together as they began a family of their own. Nathan would name their first son Alter, after his beloved father. It was a Berman tradition to name the first son Alter, which means old or eldest. This had been a great trip.

The Torah and Jewish mysticism recognize the magical power of words, especially names. The Bermans shared in this tradition. It was intended to confuse and frustrate Azriel, the Angel of Death, should he come looking to take the youngest son. The Bermans believed the angel would become confused and flustered by the name Alter and just leave, doing no harm to anyone.

The very idea made Nathan chuckle as he mused, 'This Angel of Death is not the sharpest tool in the bin, is he?'

But he would gladly continue his father's traditions with pride. They would live forward in him and in his future son, Alter, for all time.

Life could not possibly be better.

CHAPTER THIRTEEN

THE FAMILY BUSINESS

Kaluszyn, 1938

NATHAN AND FRANK RETURNED FROM WARSAW with the shearlings Nathan had purchased during his trip to Yugoslavia. As the last of the sheepskins were loaded in the storage area, the family gathered to examine the fine merchandise. "Come to the kitchen," Nathan yelled out. On the table were vodka, brandy, kielbasa, and a sack of oranges. "Oranges? Who is sick?" Mendel asked quietly. "What is the holiday?" Sam asked enthusiastically. "Yesterday Nachema agreed to become my bride. Let us eat and drink, and prepare for the grandest wedding all of Kaluszyn has ever witnessed!" Drinks were poured, happiness and laughter filled the room. Life was good.

The Berman's shearling coats were of the finest quality. People would come from all over to buy them thanks to their reputation for warmth and durability at a fair price. The business was growing steadily. The Polish government was the family's main customer, providing shearling coats for their army officers.

But there were challenges. Prime among them, the Polish government only paid twice per year. Solving this fell to Nathan. How could he maintain a steady payroll when the primary income only came twice each year? Workers outside the family had to have a regular income to buy bread for their families. They were enjoying success, but not to the point where they could stockpile large sums of money.

Nathan thought, "Why can't we print our own money?" Workers were then paid weekly with Berman Dollars, which local merchants accepted as promissory notes based on the family's reputation for honesty.

As soon as the Polish government payments came in, the Polish zlotys were exchanged for the Berman Dollars. The makeshift system worked. The business was thus able to create cash flow to grow and hire more workers.

This is one reason the Bermans had a reputation as doers not talkers. They tended to take problems head on, seeing them as challenges to solve rather than insurmountable obstacles.

CHAPTER FOURTEEN

AUTOBIOGRAPHY OF A SURVIVOR, PART IV

Poland, 1939—Joseph Berman

THE WINTER OF 1938 TO 1939 WAS A VERY COLD ONE. We had to take part in winter maneuvers, which lasted ten days. We had to be outdoors most of the time, which was very difficult.

NOTE: Joseph was drafted into the Polish Cavalry in 1937, he was twenty-two years old.

In the spring of 1939, the world political situation began to worsen. Hitler demanded that Poland give up the territory which separated the western part of Germany from East Prussia, which was part of Germany. Poland refused, and the risk of war was greater than ever. Our regiment, being stationed close to the northeastern part of Germany, or Prussia, was sent to the nearest large river called River Narev.

This was only about ten kilometers from the German border. We took positions in trenches that were still in existence from World War I. This was where the Russian army had fought with the Germans. We remained there for four or five months, building anti-tank bunkers, constructed of concrete, and renovating the old trenches in hopes of stopping the Germans in case of war.

Most people, however, did not believe that Hitler would start a war anytime soon, since the Western Allies, along with Russia, would certainly oppose the Germans if they were to attack. It was felt that the Germans would not take that risk. Unexpectedly, however, the German Foreign Minister, Von Ribentrop, arrived in Moscow.

This was probably in mid-July 1939. As a result of this event, the Polish government called for a partial mobilization. My regiment took up position along the Narev River. The weather was good and quite warm during the day and cool at night.

No one knew what Von Ribentrop was doing in Moscow, but everyone was certain that war was near. Somehow, I was not scared of that prospect. To this day, I cannot understand why. Word from home was that Nathan was returning from the Balkan countries, where he had purchased some raw materials.

At the same time, we heard that the German army had marched in to the Sudetenland, which had belonged to Czechoslovakia. A few days later, the Polish army had entered Czechoslovakia and occupied an area known as

Zaolsie, which Poland had claimed as its own for a long time.

Events were occurring at a rapid pace. We heard Hitler had met with Chamberlain, the then prime minister of England, and in hopes of preventing war, he gave all of Czechoslovakia to the Germans. In exchange, Hitler had promised that he would not attack Poland. But that promise was short lived.

On the morning of September 1, 1939, before sunrise, we were in our trenches and heard a tremendous roar of motors. On the horizon, in the sky, we saw about two dozen planes heading toward the city of Lomza. Most of my friends said the planes were ours, but I told them that they were not. Sure enough, in only a few minutes, we heard tremendous explosions coming from the direction of Lomza.

At that moment, we knew that we were at war. A few minutes later this was confirmed by a special courier who had come to our commanding officer. We were ordered into the trenches. The first day of the war nothing happened in front of our lines. It was a beautiful day with only sunshine and blue skies. But in the distance we heard the constant roar of plane engines and explosions.

After sunset, we could see on the horizon the red skies over Lomza, which was on fire. Late that night, around midnight, another soldier (who was a friend of mine) and I were assigned to patrol across the river to the northern edge of the forest. This was about two kilometers from our lines. We used a small boat to cross the river. We placed our bayonets on our rifles and quietly moved to the other end of the forest. We saw nothing and returned to our base.

Later, however, I could hear movements of trucks and tanks coming from the main road. I had a pretty good idea who they belonged to, since the Polish army did not have any motorized units. The next day, we heard conflicting reports. Some said that we were doing well, and some said the German army was all over us and we were already surrounded. The later report proved to be the more accurate one.

During the afternoon of the same day, we saw two German soldiers in the same forest we patrolled the night before. They were on bicycles and were heading for our lines. We were ordered not to fire until they were closer. When they were within range, we began to shoot.

One of them was killed instantly, and the other was seriously wounded. Our medics went to the other side of the river to help the injured soldier, and they were both brought back to our base. Later that night the other German had died. We now knew that the Germans had entered the forest and the artillery was ordered to shell the entire area.

We were on constant alert. On the third day, the Germans sent an observation plane over our position. After about an hour, they began dropping bombs on our base. The bombs were falling only a few yards from one another. It was hell, but none of them hit us directly, since our trenches were only a few yards from the river, where it curved to the north.

Minutes after the bombing stopped, I ran to the bombed-out trenches where two of my Jewish friends had been. I found bodies scattered everywhere. One friend was dead. The other, who was from Kaluszyn, was not anywhere to be found. I heard that he had escaped injury and had headed back to my trench.

Suddenly, a new wave of planes began dropping bombs. There was no time to run back to my trench, so I laid down between some trees. Bombs were falling all around me, but I was extremely lucky. After the planes were gone, I returned to my unit. We were ordered to retreat to the next forest, which was about four kilometers away.

We took all of our weapons, gear, and food. About an hour later, we all met and discovered what was left of our regiment. I found my friend from Kaluszyn and learned that all of our commanding officers had been killed in the bombings. We were then assigned to other units with a new command. You could see the confusion among the new officers. No one knew where the enemy was.

When it was dark, we began marching, not really knowing where we were headed. We could hear the constant roar of artillery, and it was not a great distance from us. Occasionally shells passed right over our heads, and we could see the sky lit up with flares.

After marching much of the night, we stopped for a couple of hours of rest. We ate some dry crackers, and had some water. One of our patrols discovered a German position, not too far in front of us. We were ordered to dig in. By daylight we had finished digging our foxholes, and to our surprise, we could see the German lines through our binoculars. Some of the Germans were walking around out in the open.

During that day, we had a few artillery and machine gun exchanges with the Germans. That night, we were ordered to retreat into the nearest forest, which in English would be called the Red Forest. We knew this forest well, since we spent a great deal of time there during our eighteen months of training.

We remained there almost until we surrendered, since we were bombed day and night by artillery fire and planes. The commander finally decided to surrender, since communication with other units of the army was lost.

I remember the white flags we hung out. When one of our patrols, carrying a white flag, approached the German lines, they were taken to the German command. The Germans ordered that the surrender take place in the marketplace of a city near the forest. There, we gave up our weapons.

Following this, I met a Jewish friend from the same regiment who was also from my hometown. We soon found out that all the stores in the marketplace belonged to Jewish merchants, and that the entire area was a Jewish neighborhood. My friend and I decided to escape, if possible, at night to the Jewish neighborhood, and change into civilian clothes and mix in with the local Jewish population.

As evening approached, we managed to slip through a very narrow street, into the Jewish section of the town. There we met a few young Jewish boys and we told them that we were Jewish and needed some civilian clothes. They tried to take us into their homes, but their parents were afraid to let us stay. Then they took us to the only synagogue in the town.

The elders in the synagogue were afraid to let us in since we were still wearing our Polish army uniforms, but the boys persuaded them to bring us clothes quickly. I can still remember the evening prayers. They told us Rosh Hashanah was only three or four days away. Soon the boys brought us clothes and shoes. They were quite shabby, and the shoes were too small.

They took our uniforms and disposed of them. The news that two Jewish soldiers were in the synagogue spread quickly through the Jewish community, and lots of people came to look at us. One woman offered us a bath and something to eat. We went with her to her home. She was a widow with two daughters about my age. She hid us in her attic and we spent the night.

She asked us to remain for Rosh Hashanah, but my friend told me that in the neighboring city of Ostrove Majowieck, which was about forty kilometers from where we were, he knew a merchant who was doing business with his brother in Warsaw. He was certain that this person would let us stay and hide for a short time, until things quieted down a bit.

We got up early the next morning and waited until the curfew was over. The Germans had established a dusk-to-dawn curfew, and no one was to be outside during the night. The woman gave us a piece of bread, and we were on our way. It was a beautiful, sunny day, but we were frightened. We were lucky, however, because most people had to walk due to the lack of transportation, and we were able to blend into the crowds. We arrived in the city about four in the afternoon.

While we were asking for directions to the main business street, we were caught by the Germans, and they took us, along with other Jews they had rounded up, to fill the craters which were made by the bombs. After a while, they let us go, and finally, we found the merchant who we had sought. When we first arrived at his home, he was extremely frightened.

After a brief conversation, however, he decided to let us stay in his attic until after Rosh Hashanah. But he insisted that we leave immediately after the holiday. We agreed, and ate and slept in the attic for three days.

On the morning after the holiday, we set off on our way toward home. We had walked down the road for only about thirty minutes when a jeep, with two German SS officers, stopped us and asked for documents, which we did not have. They made us get into the jeep and took us to a Polish army barracks in Ostrove Majowieck.

There were hundreds of Polish soldiers who had been brought there in the same way. There, they assigned us to work in a storage area which had been used by the army reserves as a changing area earlier. There we found better clothes than we were wearing. A few days later, we awoke and were ordered to stand in line. They first selected all the soldiers who were still in uniform.

Then they chose those soldiers who were in civilian clothes; and then those in civilian clothes who looked gentile. They also picked a landsman of mine who looked like a Pole. That left about seven of us who were separated from the others. Meanwhile, German army trucks began arriving. All of the soldiers and Polish civilians, including my Jewish friend (who did not look Jewish) were put on the trucks and driven away.

They locked the seven of us in the barracks jail. We were given Polish army crackers and water. They kept bringing in more suspected soldiers. Among them was a Jewish boy, about my age, who was dressed in civilian clothes. We recognized each other, since he happened to come from Wengrow, the city which I had been planning to go to. My oldest sister Hannah had married a fellow from Wengrow, and I knew his family.

Meanwhile, the German SS had begun bringing in Jews to work every morning from the city. Then, in the evening, they would take them back. They also had started using the seven of us as laborers.

My new friend and I thought this might be a chance to escape. One evening, when they began to take the Jewish workers back to the city, my friend and I snuck into the group of about seventy men, and were taken back with them. When we arrived in the city and they allowed everyone to return to their homes, my friend and I decided to leave at once for Wengrow. We had about eighty kilometers to travel, with only one hour remaining before curfew.

As we reached the outskirts of the city, we noticed a bombed-out house which was deserted. We stayed there that night. We were lucky to find some mattresses and had a good night's sleep. We were up early the next morning, but could not get started right away because of the curfew. We were very hungry.

I still had some Polish silver coins, which still could be used. Paper money was almost worthless by this time. When the curfew ended, we began walking. We saw a farmhouse, went to it, and bought some bread and milk. We knew that we would have to cross the Narev River, which was about 2,000 feet wide and very turbulent.

We asked the farmer about crossing the river and he told us that all the bridges had been destroyed by the retreating Polish soldiers, and all the temporary bridges, erected by the Germans, were well guarded. We realized that we had no choice. Neither of us could swim, and even if we could, the width and the fast rapids created a serious risk.

Each of us carried a package containing the clothes and shoes we took when we left the barracks warehouse. After we walked for a few hours, we could see one of the temporary bridges in the distance, and that it was guarded by German soldiers.

When we came to the bridge, they asked us for identification papers. We explained that we had none and they searched our packages, looking for explosives or other weapons. To our relief, they then let us cross the bridge. It is hard to describe the happiness and excitement we felt at that moment, since we then felt that getting home was a real possibility.

We still had about sixty kilometers to walk. It was a beautiful fall day. German army units on trucks were constantly passing us on the road, but they did not bother us. Then, all of a sudden, a German truck came out from a side road and stopped right in front of us. We were really frightened.

The driver got out of his truck and walked right toward us. He asked us how he could get to Wengrow, the same city to which we were headed. We told him that we were from that city and that we were going there, and that if he gave us a ride, we would direct him.

Technically, he was not supposed to give civilians a ride in his truck, but he took a chance and told us to hide under some blankets he had inside. It took only about an hour for us to get to Wengrow. The driver let us off at the outskirts of the city. As I mentioned, my friend was from Wengrow, so we went straight to his house.

When we got there, I changed into the better clothes I had brought with me and we had something to eat. My friend's parents told him not to go out, since they feared that the neighbors would see him. By this time, I was very anxious to go to my relatives and find out what was going on in Kaluszyn. My friend's parents decided that their younger daughter would take me to my relative's home.

After about a twenty-minute walk, I saw, in the distance, my sister Hannah and our brother Arie. They were outside their house, speaking with some other people. When I called their names, and they recognized me, they couldn't believe their eyes. I could see the surprised expression on their faces. They said that they must be dreaming. They could not believe that I was actually standing before them.

They told me the news from Kaluszyn. The German army had occupied the city, since it was considered a strategic location. The Polish army had concentrated a large force and surrounded the German regiment, which had been there since a previous battle. At dark, the Polish army attacked. The Germans could not retreat and they fought from house to house in the night.

By morning, about 800 Germans and as many Polish soldiers were lying in the streets and everywhere. There were also many civilian casualties, but luckily no one in our family was killed or injured.

Later, in retaliation, the German army brought hundreds of artillery pieces to the area and sent in bombers. They shelled and bombed the city mercilessly until it became a burning hell. The Polish army and the civilian population took a terrible loss. The city was under fire for several days. When it was all over, almost a thousand civilians were dead.

The Polish army withdrew and the Germans came in. I then decided that I would return to Kaluszyn the next morning. All communications were disrupted and I had no way to notify my family that I was safe and well. The only means of transportation which was available was the horse and buggy.

My sister Hannah would not allow me to travel alone, so she went along with me. The distance we would have to travel was twenty-eight kilometers, and there was great danger in the journey. The Germans could pick me up and send me to Germany as a prisoner of war. The road was full of Germans, hauling motorized vehicles captured from the Polish army, as well as trucks and buses confiscated from private citizens.

They were preoccupied, however, and did not bother us during our trip. After about six hours, we arrived at the outskirts of Kaluszyn. To play it safe, I left the buggy and walked through fields so as not to be seen by people who may have recognized me. Our house and factory were on the north side of the city, and were saved from burning by Frank, Symcha, Chaim, and others, in spite of the heavy bombardment from artillery and machine guns.

The factory was spared, but all the windows were knocked out and there were some holes from artillery shells. The warehouse inventory of finished shearling coats had already been taken by the German army administration.

Most of the homes of family members in the city and their belongings were destroyed by fire. All of my clothes, which I had left behind when I entered the army eighteen months earlier, were destroyed. I was lucky that I had taken some clothes with me while working in the warehouse of the Germans, since there was nothing to buy during this time.

The Germans did not get all of our merchandise, however. We had some inventory left in the attic of our house. We also had a store in Warsaw and an apartment, but we had no idea what had happened to the inventory, since everyone ran to Kaluszyn when the war began.

Meanwhile, the war in Poland was coming to an end since the German army was snuffing out the last remnants of resistance. The new German administration had ordered a curfew from dusk to dawn throughout Poland. In Kaluszyn, about 90 percent of the population was homeless because of the fires.

Young people began going to the east where the Russians had occupied that portion of Poland as the result of the earlier agreement between Hitler and Stalin. All of this must have taken place at the end of September or early October of 1939.

NOTE: Nathan, along with his brother Symcha, his wife, Ethel, and their children, Alter and Shia, left for Russia. Along with them went Chaim Gutarsky, the son of a local religious leader. Chaim was a bit of a character. He was active in the newly burgeoning Jewish political movements in Poland and fervently believed Communism, which was predominant in Russia, was the answer to Jewish inequality.

Symcha's motivation to leave was much more dramatic and direct. A Nazi held a Luger pistol to his head while demanding the keys to the Berman factory. Symcha later said, "I would rather eat dry bread in Russia than buttered bread in Poland under German occupation."

Initially the family found life in Russia to be quite comfortable. The men found work in the shearling business, and Ethel, ever so resourceful, discovered she could take a bottle of vodka, mix it with water and trade her low-proof concoction to the locals for food.

Back in Kaluszyn, the remaining family received word that the Nazis had reopened the factory and issued work cards to all employees. Nathan's wife, Nechema, urged him to return. Nathan quickly returned to Poland to be with his wife and young son, Alter, in Kaluszyn.

Shortly after Nathan's departure back to Poland, Chaim, Symcha, and his family were arrested as spies and sent on a very long train ride to a Siberian prison camp. Upon their arrival, the prisoners were given a simple directive. "You are 1,000 kilometers away from anything, run away and die in the forest. Here are some saws and there are the trees, if you do not wish to freeze to death you should get to work immediately."

In Kaluszyn, people began building shacks as shelter against the coming winter. Very few people had the money or resources to rebuild their destroyed homes. Our family decided that someone had to travel to Warsaw to learn the fate of our store and apartment.

Since I was the only unmarried one in the family, I was the obvious choice. One morning sometime during the end of October, my sister Hannah and I took a horse and buggy which went to Warsaw twice a week. We had to arrive there before the curfew, but the buggy broke down and caused quite a delay.

As we approached the bridge between Praga and Warsaw, we knew that the curfew was already in effect. As we crossed the bridge, a German jeep with gestapo officers stopped us. They let my sister Hannah and a few other women, as well as the driver, continue on to their destination, but took me and another man into their jeep.

They cruised around Warsaw and picked up a few more curfew violators and took us to the gestapo headquarters. This was located in the Polish Seim, which is equivalent to our senate. The building was surrounded by a very tall, steel fence in the European style. They took us to the outside garden, where ten or so other people like us had already been brought in by other gestapo patrols.

It was dark and raining, but they kept us waiting outside, with guards watching us. I was the youngest among the group. Because of the rain, the guards kept changing, perhaps once every hour. Each time they took two men away. During that time, a new guard came over to us and asked for identification.

All I had with me was a railroad pass, which allowed travel on the government railway for a two-month period. It had my picture and name on it. He checked the ID with a flashlight. He was a rather naive young German soldier. He asked me whether I was part German, because I was the only one who could communicate with him.

After a while, he came over to me and told me that every one of us was going to be shot.

This gave me the courage to attempt to escape. I was the last one in line and closest to the fence which was next to the street. There was a big tree with large branches which reached over the fence. It was pitch dark so I decided to pull myself up the tree branch and climb to the other side of the fence. I succeeded without being seen, but it was still curfew and I could not allow myself to be found wandering the streets.

I crawled on the ground until I came across a gate in front of a large building. I remained there till daylight, when I began hearing some movement on the street. I stood up and walked away. I knew Warsaw well, and knew how to get to our apartment. I walked about one and a half hours till I got home. My sister Hannah was surprised to see me and cried with happiness.

We stayed in Warsaw for a few weeks, until we sold all of the merchandise we could find. We had little contact with our family in Kaluszyn, since there was no telephone service or mail going at that time. But from time to time, some people from Kaluszyn arrived in Warsaw, and from them we found out what was going on at home.

We learned that the Germans had made the family open up the factory. Meanwhile, rumors began to circulate that the Germans were starting to build a ghetto in Warsaw.

CHAPTER FIFTEEN

THE DESTRUCTION OF KALUSZYN, MENDEL BERMAN, PART I

Kaluszyn, 1939—Mendel Berman

NOTE: MENDEL'S WRITINGS ON THE SAME GENERAL time period provide additional details and perspectives.

After the end of the war operations (after Germany attacked Poland on September 1, 1939, and occupied it within four weeks), there were immense losses in our town (Kaluszyn). Hundreds of Jews were shot and most of the houses were burned.

Due to a shortage of housing, a part of the population began to leave Kaluszyn to the adjoining towns—Morozi, Minsk-Mazowieck, Wengrow, Dobri—and also to various villages. A large number, mainly the younger people, escaped to the Russian-occupied part of Poland. Consequently, out of approximately 7,000 Jews in Kaluszyn before the war broke out, only 4,500 Jews remained there.

The first persecutions started with the capture of Jews and taking them to work. Every two to three days the Germans searched all Jewish houses and took away all valuables. This action paralyzed the entire Jewish life in our town.

When the Germans proclaimed Poland as a "General Government," the mayor of Minsk-Mazowieck was ordered to establish a Judenrat (a Jewish council appointed to represent Jews of the German-occupied territory) and immediately designated twelve persons, mainly from the former representatives of the Jewish Community Council, consisting of the following:

- Moisze Berman
- Ruben Michelson
- Abraham Gamzu
- Yudel Pienknawiez
- Moisze Kishel-Nicki
- Alter Moisze Gozik
- Yankel Goldwaser
- Leizer Bornstein
- Feldman Hershel
- Motel Arenson
- Szmuel Leizer Sadowski
- David Batalin

In addition, a Jewish police (a so-called "security service") was established under the supervision of Dembrowicz (originally from the city of Lodz) who was a cousin of Yudel Dembrowicz. Also, a Jewish Sanitation Department was created.

The first decree which the Judenrat received was to accommodate the German gendarmerie (the police force) in the occupied town, Mrozi, with everything—with painted houses, furniture, blankets, tools, and miscellaneous cookware.

In other words, they spared nothing and demanded all conveniences on our account. It went like this continuously. As soon as the Germans established new offices, the Jews were compelled to provide all necessary things. Because of these demands, the contributions increased sharply and the poverty affected all classes of the Jewish population.

In December 1939, a decree was issued that all Jews must wear white armbands with a blue Magen David emblem. For not wearing the armbands (the "shame-band," as the Germans used to call it), there would be harsh penalties. Also, the Jews were forbidden to take a train and were subjected to various other edicts.

In the first extremely cold winter of 1939 to 1940, over 1,000 Jews arrived in Kaluszyn. They were expelled from Pabianic and Kalisz—poor, frozen, many sick and small children. It is difficult to describe the awful sight. The living conditions were very bad before their arrival and now what a calamity!

These homeless people were squeezed in good-heartedly or half-heartedly (with kindness or anger). Some of them stayed in the ruined Roizman factory. Others dragged along to the neighboring villages.

It is impossible to describe the misery.

Typhoid was rampant in the Jewish population with a very high death rate. The emotions of the Jews in Kaluszyn were very depressing, but there was hope that this would not last too long.

Most people were hoping that in spring (1940) there would be an allied offensive on the western front and that the German beast would collapse. After all, England and France with the Maginot Line (an elaborate system of defense built by France against Germany after the First World War), with Belgium and Holland—this united front could liberate us.

What happened to all of these hopes is known to all of us. This was the first and painful beginning of many disappointments. In the summer of 1940, a group of Jews were taken to forced labor in the area of Janow-Podlaski, where they were mistreated for several months under very harsh conditions. Many of them returned sick and exhausted.

At the end of summer 1940, a ghetto was established with designated boundaries. There were posters with warnings put up in various places stating: "If any Jews are found outside the ghetto borders they will be shot." The conditions became increasingly worse.

The standard of living decreased gradually and Kaluszyn's Jews suffered immensely because of the severe decrees and restrictions against them.

At the beginning of 1941, the Germans started to prepare in feverish haste to attack Russia. Then the life of the Jews in Kaluszyn was transformed into hell. The distress and agony had spread with lightning speed.

Suddenly German civilians arrived wearing green hats with feathers from the infamous firm "Wolf and Goebels." Their task was to rebuild the strategic road Warszaw-Brzesc along with all bridges. All Jewish men in Kaluszyn were chased out, not sparing even the over-seventy-year-old people.

Those Jews who remained in hiding were mercilessly beaten. Many of them were sick for weeks. Afterward the Germans took all the Jews about eleven kilometers from the city, to the way of Minsk-Dobri, to remove snow from the paved road that reached several meters in height in some places. The Germans did not stop beating the workers every day.

About 600 Jews were at work and it was a rarity if one of them was not beaten. They did not spare even the ten-year-old youngsters. At the same time, the German gendarmerie shot to death Chaim "Neaman" (Chaim "the faithful") behind the city.

At the same time, the Judenrat was ordered to rebuild the internal structure of the bath house. There were rumors that the Kaluszyn Jews would be transported to the Warsaw Ghetto. A dread and fear overtook everyone. This meant the beginning of our death.

All of us had one wish: be that as it may, as long as we remain in the same place.

Unfortunately what else could the poor and emaciated Jews from Kaluszyn expect? In those days, the Jews heard the terrible news of what happened to the expelled people from the western part of Warsaw, when they were brought to the Warsaw Ghetto. Almost all of them died from starvation and epidemics.

As soon as the reconstruction of the bath house was finished, the assumed rumors became reality. A sanitary group arrived in Kaluszyn and then started with the evacuation. They emptied the Kaluszyn's school building, near the church, and converted it into an isolation place for the so-called "quarantined" (supposedly to keep them away from others to prevent the spread of contagious diseases). Every time the Germans would suddenly surround a house, they would take the people to the bath house for "delousing."

Officially it was meant that the Germans were combating typhoid. Then they started torturing the Jewish men and women physically and morally. They cut off the hair from the women and beards from the elderly men. The few meager belongings which some people were able to save in haste when they were evicted from their homes, these things were burned by the hot steam.

After the fiery hell, they were taken to the school

building near the church. Hundreds of people were squeezed inside for more than two weeks. Only some food was allowed to be brought in. It was impossible to leave that building.

Something happened there. The wife of David Psener had a sudden heart attack. There was a commotion to find a doctor. Shortly afterward, the overseer came to the sick woman and told her that she would get well soon, and then shot her to death in the cramped building among hundreds of people.

This incident brought with it panic and fear among the Jews in Kaluszyn. Not knowing the truth, if the Germans meant to "resettle" all Jews or only a part of them, the remaining Jews who were "free" people began to abandon the city wherever one could, to various neighboring towns and villages.

They were saving themselves as if they were escaping from fire. One could get out and away in the nighttime only. Every morning it was noticeable that the city became emptier from day to day. This went on for about four or five weeks.

Thus, after the last week there were almost no Jews left in the city. Only a few remained there, but they were prepared to escape from the city in the last minute.

And so it was, the Germans "cleansed" the Jewish population from typhoid by evacuating about 2,000 Jews from Kaluszyn to the Warsaw ghetto where the majority of them died from starvation and epidemics. Only a few of them succeeded in returning home through various side roads.

In those days, the Jews from Minsk-Mazoweick brought over Rabbi Naftali and the head of the Yeshiva, Tzvi Danciker, with their families, where they remained there in their city. Subsequently, Rabbi Naftali passed away and Rabbi Tzvi Danciker was savagely killed during the liquidation of the Jews from Minsk-Mazowieck on August 21, 1942.

At the same time, the war expanded gigantically.

The Judenrat was ordered to gather one hundred people for work. At that time, this was considered a miracle. Work meant so much! One could again remain in the city, even under horrible conditions.

Almost all Jews were brought in to work. Also, women and children were forced to work. All burned-out houses and both synagogues were taken apart and the building materials were transported to Janowa near Minsk where the Germans were constructing an airfield.

The school building was previously destroyed and all materials were shipped for the same purpose. The whole city was transformed into a colossal factory where all Jews were forced to crush huge piles of stones. The Nazis would not even let the dead rest in peace, on this dark and dreary morning in February, there was a fine mist in the air and a stark overcast of gloom. But no one could imagine what was to happen next. A work crew was gathered as usual and they were given heavy sledgehammers. They were told to meet at the Jewish cemetery on the outskirts of town. The task that day would be to create gravel for landing strips for the Nazi war machine. The men made their way to the graveside where their Nazi overlords made them remove the gravestones of their mothers, fathers, and grandparents, and one by one crush them to gravel.

We could not see anything except for the sky, the earth, the stones, and a mass of tormented people.

CHAPTER SIXTEEN

AUTOBIOGRAPHY OF A SURVIVOR, PART V

Kaluszyn, 1940–1942—Joseph Berman

MEANWHILE, RUMORS BEGAN TO CIRCULATE THAT the Germans were starting to build a ghetto in Warsaw. One day, I believe it was in December or January 1940, our brother Moshe arrived in Warsaw with three horse-drawn wagons, which would be used to get the raw material we still had in the warehouses. He had with him a permit from the German governor in our area. The Germans were confiscating all sheepskins in the hands of wholesalers.

My sister and I decided to leave Warsaw and return home with Moshe and the wagons. We would ride on top of the raw material. Conditions in Warsaw were already very bad, since the gestapo were picking up people at random, and they just disappeared.

Every morning, the SS came to houses and picked up the men and took them off to do all kinds of work, without giving them food. Then they would order them to return the next day or be shot.

At home, in Kaluszyn, they put our entire family to work at our factory. This was actually a privilege in those days, since we were safe from being picked up by the gestapo or other German units, which were always looking for Jews to do all the dirty work for them.

Ninety-five percent of our city had been destroyed since the beginning of the war, due to the counterattack by the Polish army around Kaluszyn. This resulted in about 800 to 900 German soldiers being killed in house-to-house fighting. In retaliation, the German command ordered the destruction of Kaluszyn by the air force and artillery. In addition, about 2,000 civilians were killed and the city was burned to the ground.

Luckily, no one from our family was killed or injured, since most of them hid in the factory which was constructed of brick. But after the bombardment was over, all of the family homes were burned down by the fire bombs, except our old home and that of Mendel. All of their belongings were destroyed as well.

The two surviving homes had been saved by family members during the bombardment. This was made possible since there was a creek running near those two homes and there was enough water to save them from burning. Everyone had to move to the old house with Frank and Fay, who had been married for six months.

Meanwhile, with all this going on at home, I was on the front line, about one hundred kilometers from Kaluszyn, fighting the German army along with my regiment. I later learned that during the bombardment and explosions, Uncle Frank and Chaim and other family members had saved our house from the fire.

As the war in Poland came to an end, and the Germans gained complete control of the country, news that the Soviet army was coming from the east caused many men and women to attempt escape to the Soviet-controlled area of Eastern Poland.

The older people began settling in neighboring towns and villages. By the winter of 1939 to 1940, the Jewish population of Kaluszyn had decreased by 50 percent from what it had been before the war.

NOTE: Some may wonder, why didn't the Jews just leave Europe and save themselves? The answer: they could not. Virtually the entire world turned its back on Jewish refugees in the late 1930s. Even the great democracies of the United States and United Kingdom refused Jewish refugees, even when it became apparent that the Nazis were intent on their extermination.

As the Nazi threat rose in the late 1930s, thirty-two European countries met in Évian, France to discuss the Jewish situation. It became clear there would be few, if any, safe havens for the Jews. The majority refused to loosen any immigration restrictions to save them.

"The world seemed to be divided into two parts—those places where the Jews could not live, and those where they could not enter."

—CHAIM WEIZMANN, FIRST PRESIDENT OF ISRAEL,
SAID ABOUT THE 1938 ÉVIAN CONFERENCE

By the end of 1940, the German governor had ordered that a ghetto be created in Kaluszyn. Posters on all roads leading out of the city warned that any Jew found outside the ghetto would be shot.

So, we became shut out from the rest of the world, with no telephones or radios, which were outlawed soon after the German occupation. The only news we heard was from the German-controlled press.

The Germans would gather Jews from Kaluszyn and force them to perform all kinds of work without pay. At night, after curfew, the Germans with the help of Polish hoodlums, would come to Jewish homes and search for valuables, taking whatever they wished. You could not complain to anyone. They were our masters during this time.

Meanwhile, as our factory started to operate again with only a few members of our family, we were saved from performing other, less desirable work such as building roads and other dirty jobs. Often, they would beat

Jews doing that and other dirty work, till they bled. Eventually, all family members were performing some type of work in the factory. Living conditions were just terrible.

Two or three families were living in one or two rooms, and sanitary conditions were unbearable. All types of contagious diseases began to affect nearly every home. The worst plague was the deadly typhoid, which resulted in hundreds of deaths.

With all this going on, our people were hopeful that when the spring of 1940 arrived, and France and Great Britain declared war on Germany, that we would be liberated.

Our factory was busy, and the Germans kept bringing in more raw material. In town, the German generals ordered the Polish mayor to form a Jewish committee, which would be responsible for delivering Jewish men to work when needed.

In addition, they would supply all the offices the Germans required in and around Kaluszyn. Spring of 1940 arrived and hopes that the Germans would be defeated by the French and British disappeared. It took the German army only five weeks to occupy all of France.

Meanwhile, in the Soviet-occupied portion of Poland, living conditions became very bad. With the influx of a few million refugees from the German-held territory, the Russians and Germans agreed to allow those refugees back from where they came.

After the ghetto was created, food and other necessities became scarce. In spite of the threat of being shot, people took risks and left the town for the farms in order to buy some food for their families. In most cases, they would leave the ghetto at night and return the next evening, after dark.

Even during those hard times, people had hope that some miracle might happen soon. Since people had no means of making a living, they had to sell their belongings in order to raise some cash to buy food. From time to time some people were caught outside the ghetto and were shot.

By early 1941, the Germans began rebuilding the main roads leading to the Soviet border. All wooden bridges were replaced with new steel and concrete structures. Most of the dirty work was being performed by Jews, without pay of course. We, who worked in the factory, were exempt from that type of labor, since we were making sheepskin coats for the Germans.

By the end of February or early March 1941, a German army truck convoy arrived in town, and every man and boy over twelve years of age was ordered to report to work, somewhere outside of town. Every house was searched to make certain that no one was left behind. Of course, if someone was hiding and was found, he would be beaten, until he bled. We felt guilty about this, and most of us in the family voluntarily reported to work with all the others.

They loaded us up on their trucks and drove us about twenty kilometers to a side road called Dobra. As we were ordered off the trucks, we saw two other vehicles filled with shovels. Everyone had to take a shovel and stand in line for orders.

We knew that we were going to shovel snow. The Dobra road had about 3 meters of snow, which remained from the winter storms. It had been an unusually cold winter, and there was very little melting. We shoveled for an entire day and night, as well as another half day, without food, until the job was completed.

We were beaten all the time with leather whips. There were 800 to 900 people on this job.

Nathan came home with a swollen face, the result of being hit by a whip. Two months later we learned the reason for the urgency of that snow removal job. The German army was preparing to attack the Soviet Union and Dobra Road was a main route for the German tanks and army to travel, they hoped, undetected. As it turned out, they were correct. By the end of May 1941, I personally counted some 1,200 German tanks passing not more than 500 feet from our house, heading for the Soviet frontier.

New hopes began to build in our minds that the Soviet army might defeat the Germans, and that they would quickly free us, since we were only forty kilometers from the Soviet border. Finally, about 3 a.m. on July 1, 1941, we were awakened by the roar of bomber engines filling the air. They were heading east toward the Soviet Union. In a short while we heard explosions, from bombs and later from artillery.

I remember that we had a creek running through our property and supposedly if you put your ear close to the water, you could hear better. So I listened to the explosions all day long, hoping that they would get closer and louder. But, to our disappointment, the sounds of battle were becoming quieter and farther away as the day passed. We knew that the Germans were winning the first battle.

For a few weeks the German press and news did not mention the location of the fighting which was taking place. All they said was that the German army had been victorious. We later learned that the Germans did not want the Russians to find out where they were, or how deeply they had penetrated Soviet territory. At this time, the Soviet army was in total chaos. After a few weeks, the Germans announced that they were eight miles from Moscow and meeting stiff resistance from suicidal Soviet units placed around Moscow. It was the general feeling that the front line had stabilized.

It was already October and the Russian winters were very cold. The Germans were not accustomed to such cold weather. Soon came an announcement that Jews had to deliver their furs to the German authorities. Since we were making sheepskin coats for the Germans, high-ranking army officers, on their way to the Russian front, always stopped at our factory and had us make them custom-fitted coats and gloves of sheepskin. They were very unhappy to be going to the Russian front.

We were preparing for another winter. We had to buy firewood since there was very little coal available. The only income people had at that time came from selling the few remaining belongings they had to the Polish farmers. With the hope of survival diminishing, the mood of the Jewish population was depressed and basically just waiting for the inevitable end.

But we again became hopeful in December 1941 when we learned that the Japanese had attacked Pearl Harbor, bringing the United States into the war. They also declared war against the Germans. Soon it was all over the German press.

By this time, all of Europe, except for Great Britain and Russia, had been occupied by the Germans, and all the people were forced to work for the German war machine.

The Germans said that it was too late for the Allies, and the two remaining countries (Britain and Russia) would soon give up the fight. Even though we had some renewed hope, we realized that it would take time, and we had no choice but to wait.

Since all of the papers were controlled by the Germans, there was no pleasure in reading the news of the war. They only wrote about the German victories on various frontiers. Whenever it was reported that they met "stiff resistance," we knew that they had suffered a big loss. It was early 1942 and we heard about the Japanese victories against the Americans in the Far East.

This was bad news for us. Meanwhile, new orders were issued for the Jews.

We heard that many communities with Jewish populations were being emptied out, and the Jews were being transported to the Warsaw Ghetto. This was very disturbing news since we knew that the Warsaw ghetto was already overcrowded and people were dying of starvation and disease, mostly typhoid.

Each day we heard more bad news. The Germans started sending Jews from Warsaw to places which were unknown. They would give each person a loaf of bread before they were taken away. Some thought they were being taken to the Russian-occupied territory.

By this time there was a panic among the Jewish population all over Poland which was almost indescribable. The transporting of the Jews from Warsaw was carried out on a daily basis, without interruption, and yet no one knew where they were being taken.

But after a few weeks, some young Jewish boys returned with the terrible news that all of those who were taken from the Warsaw ghetto were being taken to the concentration camp in Treblinka, where they were being put to death by being gassed and then burned, in the so-called crematoriums.

But no one could believe that this was actually taking place, in spite of all the brutality we witnessed by the SS and the gestapo. It took a long time to convince everyone that a death sentence was coming for every Jewish man, woman, and child.

A few months had passed and most of the Jews from the Warsaw ghetto were gone. The Germans then went to the smaller towns, outside of Warsaw, with the same purpose. Each day we would hear the names of towns from which the entire Jewish population had been evacuated. We knew that it would not take long for our city to meet the same fate. Most of our family was still working for the German army.

I recall that it was early August 1942, when a friend of mine from the neighboring city of Minsk, came to me with the bad news that his town had just been evacuated. He had escaped with his younger sister, but his parents and the rest of his family had been taken away. I took him and his sister into our home where they stayed for the next few weeks.

During this time we all believed that our situation was hopeless.

We knew that any day now our town, like all the others, would be encircled early one morning and all the Jews would be herded in the marketplace and marched to the railway station.

By mid-September, just before Yom Kippur, all the cities and towns where Jews had lived were empty. Only in Kaluszyn and Wengrow were there Jews still in the ghettos. Then, on Yom Kippur, at Kol Nidre, we all got together to pray in a room located in our factory.

I don't think it is possible to describe the tension and dread we felt at that time, looking at each other, knowing that soon we would all die by different means.

Then, on the second night of Yom Kippur, a few Jewish boys managed to escape from the encirclement of Wengrow and told us that their town was being evacuated of all Jews.

CHAPTER SEVENTEEN

THE DESTRUCTION OF KALUSZYN, PART II

Kaluszyn, 1941–1942—Mendel Berman

ON JUNE 22, 1941 THE GERMANS STARTED THE WAR
against Russia—a blitzkrieg in the darkness. This gave us
a spark of hope for a speedy liberation. Since we were so
close to the Russian border, we hoped that a great miracle
would occur.

But, unfortunately, instead of help and liberation, we
were bitterly disappointed. The powerful German war
machine attacked the Soviet Union ferociously. This was
the beginning of darkness over the entire Eastern Europe.
For a short time we were at the midpoint of the calamity.

We heard the rattling sounds in the "renewed Europe"
about the Jewish "tubercular microbe." Goebbels (the
German propaganda minister) and Schtreicher (a high-
ranking Nazi minister) proclaimed that the Jews must

disappear from Europe. Thus, we were the lowly from the lowliest!

In autumn of 1940, the Kaluszyn Jews were apathetic and hopeless. Again these Jews were tormented and tortured ceaselessly at the machines that crushed hundreds of meters of stones. Along with the stones, the last Jewish hopes were being crushed into bits. In those days when we reminisced of the years before the war, it seemed like a vanished dream, never to return again.

In the beginning of winter of 1942, it was bitterly cold. There came an order under the threat of being shot that all of the Jews must give up all garments made of fur within several days. We could no longer see any Jew wearing a fur jacket or a fur coat.

At the end of winter there were rumors that, in the area of Poland annexed to the Third Reich, the Germans were conducting gas experiments on the Jews. The air was filled with such rumors, but the majority of us could not believe that those rumors were true.

In April 1942, we received other bad news: that in a certain night in Warsaw the German SS (the policing unit of the German army) shot to death a great number of Jews, among them the Kaluszyn Bund organization leader, Moishe Goldberg, with his wife, Rochtshe Lis.

Also, that all Jews in Lublin were deported to an unknown destination. We heard also that the SS had arrived in other cities with lists ordering all Jews to assemble. Afterward, all of them were shot.

In May 1942, we heard persistent rumors that all Jews in the occupied Russian territories would be taken to different work units. Thus such rumors were being spread and in the meantime, we carried the stones from all sides and the stone factory ran continuously. They did not even let the dead rest in peace.

They removed the stone fence from the old cemetery along with the tombstones. Then they planted potatoes in the empty field. Also, they took away the tombstones from the new cemetery. Thus the destruction was spreading with a dreadful haste.

NOTE: Crushing of stones is mentioned by both Mendel and Joseph in several places. They are referring to a factory set up by the Nazis to use crushed stone to build military-grade roads. Even the tombstones from Kaluszyn's Jewish cemeteries were desecrated and crushed for this purpose.

In July 1942, great masses of Jews were deported from the Warsaw Ghetto. In the beginning we did not know where they were taken to. We were told that they would be resettled in the occupied Russian territories. But the Jews in Kaluszyn, as well as in other places, had agonizing thoughts: where was the destination for the hundreds of thousands of the Warsaw Jews?

And finally the puzzle was clear. It was the beginning of the end of the last act of our tragedy. All Jews knew then that this was the beginning of the massive annihilation of the entire Jewish population in the infamous extermination factory, Treblinka.

What could one do? Where could one escape? All of us felt like being in a closed cage without any recourse or hope. The Polish population was threatened with death for helping Jews. It is difficult to express what went on in the Jewish hearts, being confronted with an impending death.

A particularly horrible pain overwhelmed us, seeing the tragedy of our children. Regardless of age, they understood and felt what was happening. When looking in their innocent eyes, a bitter and just anger cried out at us! Why? What was the purpose for creating us? And our eyes responded: you are so right.

Regarding the chapter of our destruction, all kinds of thoughts enter my mind! How can one find words that can describe the torment in one's heart and the pain in one's soul? No, I am unable to compose any words which could express the sorrow and agony in our hearts and souls with regard to the torture and suffering of our children.

Thus, we found ourselves in a sinking ship. Everyone was looking for a way how to save oneself, even grasping at straws.

Again, more news: the deportation of the Jews from Warsaw had stopped. All working people stayed in the city. Because of this news there was a sudden rush (of remaining survivors) to attach themselves to the working groups.

In the meantime, the extermination machine was running according to a strategic plan. During the second half of August 1942, the Jews from Otwock and Rembertow were expelled. Some optimists were comforted by the fact that these cities belonged to the district of Warsaw. On August 21, 1942, the Jews from Minsk-Mazowieck were also deported.

The Angel of Death stood at our door.

On August 22, 1942, there was an alarming stampede. The extermination squad arrived here (in Kaluszyn). It seemed that they bypassed Kaluszyn until that time. On the same day, the remaining Jews were deported from Siedice (TRANSLATOR'S NOTE: I didn't have the Yiddish and I'm not sure if this is Siedice, a neighboring town or Siedlec, as provided in English which is in Western Poland), Mezricz, and other towns.

THE LIVING ENVY THE DEAD

September 1942: we had already awaited our death in the last two months. Being totally resigned, we chatted with one another. "Let there be ten minutes after everything," (after death). Let there be an end once and for all. My uncle, a mortician, told me that when somebody died there, then, after saying, "Blessed be thou for your righteous deeds," the mortician would say, "Mazel Tov," since that person was buried like a human being. Thus, the living people would envy the dead ones.

And the last Yom Kippur had arrived here in Kaluszyn. On that day there were horrible scenes. Several hundred Jews were taken to work to Jezorek, a few of them were shot to death. Also, in the evening, Moishe Kiszelnicki was shot. It was apparent to us that these were our last days. Whoever still had courage tried to escape to the camps of Miene, Kuflew, Jezorek, Lenk, and Sucha.

On the following day, after Yom Kippur, the Germans started with the deportation of the Jews from Wengrow. All Jews from the vicinity of Kaluszyn, from Mrozi, Dobri, Latawicze, and adjoining villages—all of them were brought to Kaluszyn.

On September 1942, Friday, on the eve of Sukkot, when it was still dark, Kaluszyn was surrounded by hundreds of German gendarmes and Polish police, and terrible shootings pierced through the city from all sides. It was the beginning.

In the early morning, the gendarme units walked from house to house. All Jews were being dragged out and taken to the marketplace. Those people who were sick and were not able to leave were shot in their homes. Whoever was trying to escape was shot. People were being thrown out from the attics and Jewish blood spilled from all sides. This ("action") lasted eight days.

Every day there were "funerals" for living people who were then taken to the cemetery. About 1,000 Jews were shot in that graveyard.

After this action against the Jews, the gendarmes

(with their collaborators) started compiling an inventory. All those things which remained in the Jewish houses were sold out. This sale had an innocently sounding name: "Bought during the cheap week" (alluding to the Jewish disaster). Also, many houses were sold and then taken apart.

And we too must help with the destruction of the Jewish homes!

A deadly silence permeated the old (bygone) and homey city of Kaluszyn which looked like an abandoned cemetery. Bibles and books were scattered on the streets, photographs of so many dear and familiar people. When I looked at such scenes, I felt as if the souls of the decimated people were flying around in the dark desert.

Only a few small islands (camps) were still left where some Jews remained there. They were the several camps located in the villages nearby Kaluszyn-Miene, Kuflew, Jezorek, Lenk, and Suche. Every night some people from these villages would come to Kaluszyn hoping to be able to get into the dwelling houses of their relatives so that they could retrieve something which was concealed in the abandoned hideaways. Thanks to those people, we still had some contact with the so-called "islands." Every day we heard that some people were shot here and there, and all of them at their working place.

And so it lasted until November 1942. Then, again, Kaluszyn was declared as a ghetto, where they started to concentrate all Jews from the above-mentioned camps. It was announced that all Jews, wherever they were, could freely come to the ghetto of Kaluszyn. But the first group of Jews from Kuflew's camp who bypassed Mrozi with the intention to reach the ghetto, all of them, about ninety Jews, were shot there.

Finally, the second ghetto was put together. The suffering there was indescribable. A great number of those people were not normal anymore. Many of them were blind, hungry, raggedy, dirty, and unshorn. These people were squeezed into the dilapidated buildings, without leaving any empty spaces.

CHAPTER EIGHTEEN

AUTOBIOGRAPHY OF A SURVIVOR, PART VI

Kaluszyn, 1942—Joseph Berman

THERE WAS NOTHING THAT ANYONE COULD DO. The next morning I was standing inside of the barbed wire fence, which enclosed our ghetto, when a man by the name of Stanislaw Boruc came to me and told me that he had witnessed the events in Wengrow the night before. We had known this man for many years. We used to make sheepskin coats for him and his family.

As a matter of fact, his father, who was still living, had been a good friend of my father, going back to World War I. During our conversation, he told me that if the Germans came after us, we could come to his farm, and he would do whatever he could to help us. He gave me a loaf of bread and left. We finally had a spark of hope. I ran to the house to tell everyone the news. We began to make plans.

We took two big glass jars and filled them with all the jewelry, gold and American dollars we collected from every member of the family. We sealed them with paraffin, the compound which is used in making candles, and I buried them in the back of our factory that night. I told everyone in the family the exact location I had chosen.

RIGHTEOUS POLES

NOTE: Stanislaw Boruc, his wife, Teofila, and son, Czelaw, were awarded by the Institute of Yad Vashem with the title "Righteous Among Nations of the World" in November of 1992.

The Boruc family played a crucial role in the Bermans' story going forward. They were a great blessing for the Berman family. Arguably, the Bermans would be bereft of any hope if it were not for the courage and generosity of the Borucs. Indeed, many who are alive today would not be.

People like this remind us that, even if the vast majority of others around us are savage, hateful, or simply indifferent, there are always some good people with the compassion and heart to do the right thing—regardless of personal risk.

From Wikipedia:

Polish Righteous Among the Nations: The citizens of Poland have the world's highest count of individuals who have been recognized by Yad Vashem of Jerusalem for saving Jews from extermination during the Holocaust in World War II.

We prepared tools to take with us, just in case we were loaded into cattle cars with no openings. Our plan was to break the wall of the car and escape by jumping from the speeding train.

Only a few days later, after the evacuation of Wengrow, we learned that on the following morning, the deportation of Kaluszyn would begin. At that time there were still a few forced labor camps located not far from our city, and some younger Jews were working for the Germans under guard of the militia. When the news reached our ghetto, many young men and women ran away, at dawn, to those labor camps.

Among them were my sisters Fay and Chaya (with her little girl), also my brother Arie's wife and son of about six or seven. They ran away because everyone believed that, even if the Germans allowed the factory workers to remain behind, the women would certainly be taken away. So they ran to Mienie, about fifteen kilometers from Kaluszyn.

And so it was, the next morning while it was still dark, the Germans, the Polish police, and the Polish firefighters, who the Germans had ordered to assist them, had already encircled the town.

They ordered everyone to get to the marketplace

where they were to be concentrated. Our factory manager, a gentile and the son of a neighbor, tried to talk the Germans into allowing us to stay at work since there were still many leather and sheepskin coats to be finished. But the Germans did not have the authority to change their orders. So, we along with the other Jews, were taken to the marketplace.

We remained there for several hours. Finally, our factory manager had been able to convince Germans with higher authority to allow us to return to the factory to finish the raw materials. Before we had left for the marketplace, we had hidden most of the women and older couples in the attic of our old house.

Among them were our oldest sister, Hannah, with her thirteen-year-old son and Frank's father and mother. Also hidden there was my oldest brother, Yakov, who was about sixty years old, with his wife, and the parents of my brother-in-law, Isaac.

For a few nights I brought them food. Finally, however, they were discovered and were taken to the city jail along with many other men, women, and children who had been hiding. Eventually they were taken to the Jewish cemetery where they were shot and killed.

NOTE: It was during this time that Nathan looked up from the factory floor to see his beloved wife, Nechema, and son, Alter, among the women, children, and elderly men being led away on the catwalk above the floor to their deaths.

Nechema looked down toward Nathan and said, "This is the end for us."

They were all murdered—shot and thrown into a mass grave near the outskirts of the ruined Jewish cemetery.

One can only try to imagine the sickening horror and helplessness Nathan felt as he looked up and heard the fateful comment of his beloved wife. His son, Alter, named after his father and Berman family tradition, also perished.

Also among the Berman family murdered that day:

- Yankel and wife, Yospe, and five children
- Moishe and wife, Tzinka, and four children
- Hannah and husband, David, and son, Alter
- Arie and wife, Gretel, and son, Alter
- Chaya and husband, Itzak, and daughter, Sarah

It was the end of September, or early October of 1942. We were still working in the factory, while there remained some unfinished raw material. The war on the Russian front was at a stalemate. We had heard, from secret sources, that the German army, after a few months of battle for Stalingrad, had suffered a tremendous defeat and that there were tens of thousands of casualties, as the result of house-to-house fighting in that city. Of course, this gave us some comfort, but the battle was taking place about 2,000 kilometers from us.

We were getting messages from the members of our

family who were at the labor camps in Miernia. One day we learned that our brother Arie's wife was killed by some sort of shooting.

The month of October was very warm for that time of year. This was good for the Jews who had worked in the labor camps outside of the city since they had been digging drainage trenches for irrigation in the marshy fields, in order to make the land drier. But by November it became very cold and there was snow and frost, which is typical for Poland.

By the beginning of December, the Germans began liquidating the few remaining labor camps located outside of the city, and formed a new ghetto in Kaluszyn for those Jews. There were only about a thousand of them, mostly young people.

Among them were our sisters Fay and Chaya, with her little girl, Sarah; also, our brother Arie's little boy, Alter. They had all been hiding in the labor camps, and the Germans had not discovered them.

We all knew that this was the last concentration of Jews who were still alive in the area. The month of December began very cold with lots of snow.

DEATH TRAIN TO TREBLINKA

On the morning of December 9, we were awakened by knocks on the doors and told to get dressed and report to the marketplace, or be shot. I remember my brother

Mendel's older daughter (she was eighteen years old), who had escaped the first evacuation to the death camp, Treblinka, by hiding on some farm since September. She had just come back home, only to be trapped again. She ran away, just as she had done the first time. We did not know if she had made it.

It was still dark when we began walking to the marketplace, as ordered. People from all sides began to arrive. We were ordered to sit down in the snow. It took a few hours until we were ordered to start walking to the railroad station called Mrozy, which was almost about five kilometers from Kaluszyn.

They first took all the children away. They were never seen again, not even on the train. On the way to the railroad station, we were guarded by the German SS, the Polish police, and firefighters from Kaluszyn. Most of the people were already physically and psychologically defeated, without any will to escape or fight for survival.

Everyone had hoped for a miracle, as had happened in the teachings of the Bible. But there was no miracle. That march took about one and one-half hours. We arrived at the railroad station and there was no train waiting for us. Again they ordered us to sit in the snow. We sat there, without food or water. Finally, at about 6:30 in the evening, a train arrived. There were many cattle cars attached.

CHAPTER NINETEEN

THE DESTRUCTION OF KALUSZYN, PART III

Kaluszyn, 1942—Mendel Berman

IT DID NOT, HOWEVER, LAST LONG. ON DECEMBER 9, 1942, all 2,500 people were deported from Kaluszyn. We were chased to Mrozi, accompanied by shootings around us. The wagon train already awaited us. We were packed into the wagons and were transported to Treblinka (an extermination camp in Poland).

Thus, the destruction of Kaluszyn came to an end.

NOTE: Mendel's writings end at this time frame. For many if not most Jews, this was the literal end. But for some, it was not. Mendel, a survivor, ends his recollections here, but carries on in the fight to survive with his brothers Joseph and Nathan, sister Fay and brother-in-law, Frank, in the countryside of Kaluszyn.

Mendel's two daughters also escaped the death camp, but eventually succumbed to disease.

CHAPTER TWENTY

AUTOBIOGRAPHY OF A SURVIVOR, PART VII

Kaluszyn, 1942—Joseph Berman

WE WERE PREPARED WITH SMALL TOOLS, WHICH would help us break a wall in the train car, if necessary. Some people tried to run away before entering the trains, but they were immediately shot. It took about one and a half hours until we were all packed into train cars.

Everyone knew that in a few hours we would arrive at the death camp, Treblinka. Most of our family wound up in the same cattle car. The cars were so packed that you could hardly reach into your pocket. We managed to push ourselves to the corner of the car, where a small opening near the top was made available for the animals to get some air.

NOTE: The family had heard from other Jews who managed to escape earlier that there was a way out of the cattle cars. They would find an air vent and, using the screwdriver they secreted onboard, pry it loose.

To our surprise, that opening of about fifteen inches by twelve inches, was not sealed off. It was about 8:00 p.m. and we felt the train begin to move. Since my brother Nathan was the closest to the opening, we helped him up to the window. He had to go through feet first. It had traveled no more than a few hundred yards, and he jumped.

Frank was right behind him. He jumped. In front of me was a distant relative of ours, Burach Baranek. I tried several times to get him to jump, but he was too frightened. By that time the train had hit full speed. I told him to let me through, to the opening. I got help from several others, and managed to get my feet out, and then I jumped.

NOTE: Sister Fay and her husband, Frank, jumped after Nathan. Mendel, Joe, and then finally nephew, Sam, also jumped. But since Sam jumped last, he wound up closer to the Russian border.

It seemed that I had landed on a boulder and was knocked unconscious. When I awoke, I looked at my watch. It was 11:30 p.m. I had been out for three hours. A strange thing had happened while I laid by the tracks. I thought that I had been dreaming that a train had gone by.

But it had been true. Several trains had gone by while I had laid there, unconscious. I stood up and looked around, and remembered what had happened. I was cold and had lost my hat, which I always wore at that time.

I noticed a light in the distance and I decided to follow it. When I got closer, I noticed that it was a farmhouse. When I got even closer, two dogs began barking at me. After a while, the farmer came out and asked me where I came from. When I told him, he seemed to know all about it. He was surprised that I had survived the cold. I asked him where this place was and he told me it was about eighteen kilometers from the train station where I had begun my journey. He seemed to be nice, but you never knew. But at that point, I did not have much choice but to trust him.

I could not tell him where I was going, but I knew the main road from which I could find my way. I asked him if I could pay him for his kindness, and if he would take me to the main road.

From there I could find my way to the Borucs' home, where any of us who survived were to meet. In fact, he was a very kind person. He invited me into his house and brought me a piece of bread and some milk. He told me that I should not go alone if I did not know this area, since there was a German air patrol station nearby. They operated the air traffic control for the German air force.

He agreed to take me to the main road I had asked about. He brought in a sack of hay for me to lay down in and get some sleep, and he told me to wake up about four in the morning and he would take me. In addition to the risk of Germans, he warned me that there were many fish ponds in the area which were slightly frozen and covered with snow. It would have been very easy for someone not familiar with that area to fall in. At that point I agreed.

The next morning, while it was still dark, he woke me and we both walked for a long time through fields covered with a great deal of snow. It was still dark when we reached the main road I had been seeking. From that point I was on my own, but I knew which direction I needed to go. As I did not intend to walk during daylight, I quickly headed for the nearest farm. I noticed a man already doing some work in his barn. As I came closer, I recognized him as a Jew from Kaluszyn. He used to work for us in our factory before the war.

When he saw me, he called me into the barn. He had recognized me immediately. I told him what had happened, and that I had jumped from the train. I told him that I did not want to walk during the daylight hours. He went into the farmer's house and asked the farmer if he would allow me to stay until the following evening.

He agreed, on the condition that I help them through the day with various chores. He gave me some food, which I could not eat, even though I was very hungry. As I worked, I wondered what had become of Nathan and Frank. Had they arrived at the Boruc farm safely? I asked the farmer how far it was to the village I was heading for. He said it was only about three kilometers away.

I asked him if one of his sons could take me to that village after daylight. I offered to pay him and he agreed.

About four, it started to get dark outside. The farmer's son and I began to walk.

After about an hour, we arrived at the village. He asked me where I was going, but I would not tell him the truth. I told him I was to meet my brother by the water mill. He showed me which direction to take and I gave him some money, and he left.

A short time later, I approached the house next to the windmill and knocked at the door. An older woman opened the door and asked me what I wanted. I asked her if this was the house where the Borucs lived. When she answered yes, I told her who I was. She told me that Nathan and Frank were inside, having arrived around midnight. I went inside, and we embraced. They asked me where I had been during the past twenty-four hours, and I told them my story.

CHAPTER TWENTY-ONE

MARTYRDOM, RESISTANCE, AND DESTRUCTION

* * *

"...THE GERMANS, WHO ENTERED TOWN FROM A FEW directions (mainly via the Węgrów road) fortified themselves in a number of localities around town—near Bermans' factory close to the river and in the (Christian) cemetery, where the brick fence...

...Meanwhile the Volksdeutche Sieradzinski, who took over the management of the pelisse factory of Berman and Gozhik, demanded that a few dozen men that he needed to produce pelisses for the German army be left in town. Among those were: Alter Gozhik, the best expert in the factory, the three brothers Berman, with their sister and brother-in-law (Frank) Radzinski.

Incidentally, the factory did not function long. As soon as the work was completed, the manager Sieradzinski delivered his thirty Jews for deportation. Some of them jumped from the train on the way to Treblinka: one went to the partisans in the forest, the three brothers Berman with their sister and brother-in-law, Radzinski hid in a bunker.

In the afternoon, the people were driven to the railway station at Mrozy (men on foot, women and children were loaded onto wagons like luggage). The Germans rode on horseback, driving the crowd and shooting all the while; the entire road was covered in bloodstains.

In Mrozy, a freight train was waiting for the Kaluszyn transport. Everybody was squeezed into the wagons the floors of which were covered with lime. Many people choked to death as soon as they entered the wagons. Many (including women) jumped from the death train that was speeding to Treblinka.

Most of those that jumped were shot by the Nazis guarding the transport, or captured by Poles and handed over to the Germans. Thus, for instance, a boy that jumped from the train together with Abraham Wyezhba sustaining a leg injury was killed by a bullet fired by a Pole close to the forest. Some individuals that managed to survive went to the Camp Sucha where they worked for a while for the poretz (non-Jewish landowner, nobleman G.G.) until he was ordered to send them to Kałuszyn. As soon as they arrived they were rearrested and taken to the train.[4]

---

4   Yosef Kermish and Gooter Goldberg, translator, "Martyrdom, Resistance and Destruction of the Jewish Community in Kaluszyn: The Annihilation Process; Final Destruction of the Community" from *The Memorial Book of Kaluszyn* (Tel Aviv, 1961).

CHAPTER TWENTY-TWO

AUTOBIOGRAPHY OF A SURVIVOR, PART VIII

Kaluszyn, 1942–1944—Joseph Berman

NOTE: WE ARE PICKING UP JOSEPH'S NARRATIVE AT a time when Nathan, Fay, Frank, Mendel, and Joseph have reunited at the Boruc family farm after escaping the train to Treblinka.

They told me that they met after only a few minutes, after jumping off the train. They had met a few more boys from Kaluszyn who had also jumped from other cattle cars. They had decided to walk back to the city, since they knew how to get to the Boruc farm from there. My brother Mendel arrived two days later. His younger daughter came one day after that. It took my sister Fay six days to get to the village and join us.

THE BORUCS, LEADERS OF THE UNDERGROUND, SHELTER THE BERMANS

The Boruc family wondered what our plans were. We told them that we wanted to wait a few more days in case more members of our family had jumped off the train, and might be lost somewhere. But no one else showed up. We knew that we could not stay there too long.

The Borucs told us that they had some connections, and that we could stay with some people they knew, but that we would have to pay them. We did not have any money with us and felt that it was too risky to return to our factory in Kaluszyn and get the valuables we had buried there. The factory, we knew, was well guarded by the Polish police.

We decided to contact one of our former Polish workers, who we thought was a very honest man. During the time of the German occupation, he had been very close to us and had helped us when he could. We decided that a member of the Boruc family would go to Kaluszyn on a market day (which was each Tuesday) when farmers would come to the city to sell their produce to the residents.

At the same time, the farmers would buy goods they needed for their farms. We thought that it would not look suspicious if Mr. Boruc would go into the city and meet our former employee, Mr. Kaczorek. During the past few months we had given him many of our household items, such as clothes, linens, feather blankets. Usually this was done at night.

We gave Mr. Boruc the address and directions to Kaczorek's house. We had also hoped that we could retrieve some of the clothes we had given him. So on the next Tuesday, Mr. Boruc went to Kaluszyn. When he returned that evening, he had with him Mr. Kaczorek and his wife. They were very happy to see us, since they knew we had all been taken away.

The Boruc family made dinner for all of us. After we ate, we told Kaczorek about the money and jewels we had buried by the factory, and that with this money we might have a chance to survive the war. We explained that we would have to pay people for taking the risk of hiding us.

We also told him that the Boruc family were leaders in the underground movement in this area, and that they would find places for us to hide. But we would still have to pay. We decided that Mrs. Kaczorek would have to be the one to retrieve the jars, since only women would come to the creek which ran through our property between the factory and our house, in order to wash their laundry. A man going there would be immediately suspected.

We assured her that the police were only on guard at the front gate entrance to the factory. We told her that if she watched for a time, till no one else was doing their laundry and then pretended that she had to go to the bathroom, behind the factory where the jars were buried, she would not be noticed. I told her exactly where to find the treasure, and that it was buried only about ten inches deep.

The Kaczoreks then returned to Kaluszyn. We took a great risk in confiding in them. They could take the money and jewels for themselves, and come up with many excuses. Either they could claim that they did not locate the jars, or that they were already gone, or that someone had caught her and taken them from her by force. We waited anxiously for them to return. The Borucs could not believe that we had trusted these people. We also had great doubts.

But they surprised us all. After only two days, they showed up with everything still intact. They had not even attempted to open the jars. We gave them some money and they returned to their home. We had opened the jars in front of the entire Boruc family, and told them that we had no more. We gave everything to the son who had come to the factory and offered us refuge in case of a crisis.

NOTE: Survivors in the Kaluszyn countryside include:

- Nathan (brother)
- Joseph (brother)
- Mendel (brother) and his two daughters:
- Manya and her older sister, Lecha
- Fay (sister) and her husband, Frank

They went right to work, seeking places for us to hide; either all together or separately. The farmer who had been sheltering Mendel's younger daughter, agreed to take in Mendel and his younger daughter as well, since we agreed to pay him. Two days later they found a place for me, Nathan, Frank, and Fay. But they told us that it was quite a distance away and we would have to travel there by night. The same evening, at sundown, a wagon drawn by two horses and loaded with farm equipment arrived. When it became very dark, we all climbed onto the wagon and hid under the hay they had prepared for us.

We rode till after midnight. When we stopped we were taken into a house in a small town. After a day or two we realized that this was a very risky place to stay. We let the Borucs know this and explained why we did not feel safe. So, two days later we were back with the Boruc family, arriving in the same wagon we had left in.

When we arrived there, they told us that they had found another place, but only for two of us. Frank and Fay left for that location the next day. They went to stay with a Polish family which had been deported by the Germans from the western part of the country, which had been declared as part of German territory.

A few days later, they found a place for Nathan and me. Again, we felt that this was not a safe location. It was on a farm, and we were put in the barn. There was already a fugitive there, a Soviet P.O.W. who had escaped from a German prison camp. He would come in to the barn in the evening. We did not like the situation at all.

When we complained to the farmer, he took us to a potato mound outside. It was cold and just impossible to live in that spot. We asked him if he had another place for us, and he said he would take us into the house. He had two grown daughters, the older one had a boyfriend. We did not like this arrangement either.

We wanted to see Mr. Boruc. It was the day before New Year's Eve. We made arrangements with a young boy who worked for the farmer to take us to the outskirts of the village one night, where the Boruc family live. We had about ten kilometers to walk, through frozen fields, covered with one inch of freshly fallen snow.

It took us about two hours to get there. We paid the boy for the favor, and he left us. It was already quite late when we found the house. We knocked, and when Mrs. Boruc opened the door, she was surprised to see us. We told Mr. Boruc about the place we had stayed, and he agreed that it was probably not very safe. We told him that we wanted to go and see Mendel and his two girls. He told us to stay overnight, and that we could leave the following evening.

We had about three kilometers to travel to the farm where Mendel was staying. It was New Year's Eve, 1942. When we arrived, we saw only a barn. We knocked, but no one answered. We realized that they were probably afraid to answer, not knowing who was there.

Then, quietly, we began calling their names in Yiddish. They then came to the door and opened it. They told us that they were frightened, since the farmer had left for the winter. He had told them that if they were caught he would deny any knowledge of them. We stayed with them in the barn, there being five of us now.

Every few days we would go to the Boruc farm for some bread, cheese, and water. It was very difficult to survive under these conditions, especially since it was such a cold winter. One day, the farmer returned to see if Mendel and his daughters were still alive. When he saw the rest of us, he was very surprised. We told him that we would pay him extra money to let us all stay in his barn.

We knew, however, that with this extremely cold weather that it would be impossible to survive there for the entire winter. We asked him if we could build a wooden shack in the front of the barn, with one double wall and an entrance through a small basement, which would be filled with potatoes. And if there was any danger, we could go through the basement and into the double wall.

We suggested that the farmer could then fill the basement with sacks of tomatoes. This way, he could tell his neighbors that he had built the shack because his barn was always being broken into, and his grain was being stolen. He liked the idea, and we gave him money to buy lumber and other building supplies.

As it turned out, he was a very handy person and he built the entire shack all by himself. Within a few weeks it was completed and we had a new place to live, complete with a wood-burning stove. We could now boil water and cook soup. It was like a godsend for us.

The farmer stayed with us most of the time. On occasion he would go to his other farm for a few days at a time. Once he left for the weekend, but did not return as expected. Later, his son came and told us that there had been a typhoid epidemic in the village and that more than half of the population was infected, including our farmer.

This was very bad news for us. We would not be able to make a fire, since the smoke would be suspicious. Everyone knew that the farmer was very ill, and staying at his other farm. This happened around the end of February 1943.

Shortly after we heard this news, Nathan and I left one night to go to the Borucs and tell them about our new situation. On the way, we spotted a farm located between two villages. We both felt that this would be an ideal place to stay. There did not seem to be any neighbors around. We decided that when we met with Mr. Boruc, we would ask him about this farm and what kind of people lived there.

As it turned out, Mr. Boruc knew the farmer. His name was also Boruc, and the farm was actually called a "colony" since there were no other farms within several kilometers in any direction. We told Mr. Boruc that we would stop by this colony on the way back and talk to the farmer.

When we approached the farm, two dogs began barking at a distance. We always carried big sticks at night because of dogs. As we came closer, the barking became more intense. The farmer finally came out to see why the dogs were barking. As we approached him, we asked him if we could buy some food. He was not surprised to see some young Jews wandering about at night looking for food.

He was surprised, however, that we had money to pay for the food, since most of the other Jews had to beg for it.

He invited us into the house and complimented us for still being well dressed and in good condition. He seemed to be very nice, and we told him that we had just lost our hiding place, due to the illness of the farmer we had been staying with. We asked him if he would be interested in letting us stay with him. We told him we would pay him well.

He hesitated in giving us an answer. We tried to convince him that this would be a perfect place for us since there was no one living near him. We thought that he might be interested in our proposition, but he told us to come back in two nights, since he wanted to talk it over with his wife and two sons, who were not home at the time. We, of course, told him that there were five of us: three men and two girls. We then returned to our so-called "home," the shack we had been living in.

We told Mendel the whole story, telling him there was a chance we might have a new place to stay. The second day after we had returned to the shack, the farmer's son arrived and informed us that his father had died a few days earlier. He said that we would have to go and find a new place to stay. We told him that we would need only a few more days, and that we would then be able to go, and he agreed.

The next day after dark, we returned to the Boruc colony. He told us that he would be willing to take in the three men, but that Mendel's daughters would have to stay with his younger brother, who lived in the village. This was very good news to us, and we felt that this was our lucky day.

We could start to relax and wait till the German army would be defeated. During this time they had suffered their first major defeat at the battle in and around Stalingrad. This had also given hope to the people who were trying to help us, and improve their chances for survival.

So the next day, the three of us came to live in the colony and Mendel's daughters went to the village to stay with Boruc's brother. During the day, we stayed in the barn. At night, we would come to the house and have dinner with their family, and warm up a bit from the cold conditions of the barn. At night we slept in the stable where it was warmer because of the cows, pigs, and horses. But the smell was so terrible that we decided to go back to the barn to sleep.

We were still not happy with the security of these new accommodations, so the next day we called one of the sons into the barn and suggested that we might build a bunker in the ground with an entrance from the barn, so that in the case of an emergency, we could crawl into the bunker and camouflage the entrance. He liked the idea and went to discuss it with his parents and brother. They also liked the idea, so the next day the boys began to dig in a hurry, so that no one would see what they were doing. The bunker was built outside, next to the barn, with an entrance in the barn, as we had suggested. We not only felt safer, but it was also quite a bit warmer than the barn. It was already March of 1943, and we were much more relaxed. Our hopes for surviving the war were also much higher than they had been in a long time.

During the day, we spent our time underground in the bunker. At night we would come out into the fresh air and do some walking around the farm, but always watching out for any danger. From time to time, we would meet with Mr. Boruc, during the night, of course, and he would bring us money, which we needed to pay the farmer. We also needed money for food, for Frank and Fay, and for Mendel's girls.

And so, as time passed and we remained at this location, we would hear reports from the underground about the various defeats of the German army, on the Russian front and also in North Africa, where the British army, led by General Montgomery, had broken through the German lines taking thousands of war prisoners. They were in full retreat from Libya and Tunisia to Algeria.

On the Russian front, the Germans had already admitted defeat at Stalingrad where they had lost about one-half million soldiers, either killed or taken prisoner.

They had to retreat about 500 kilometers west of Stalingrad. Of course, that was the kind of news we had all been waiting for.

At that time, the only Jews left were about 30,000 in the Warsaw ghetto, where they did some work for the German army. Most of them were young and all of them knew what fate was awaiting them. They prepared themselves for a fight which they knew they would certainly lose. But they would rather die in battle than in the gas chambers.

Then it came, on the first day of Passover in 1943. The Germans, as they usually did, picked a Jewish holiday for their actions against them. They had ordered everyone to come out of the ghetto. They were met with gunfire. The Germans retreated for a time, but came back with armored vehicles.

But this time they were met with firebombs, causing many of the vehicles to burn. Many Germans were killed. Then the Germans brought in the air force, turning the Warsaw ghetto into an inferno.

As we were only about fifty-six kilometers from Warsaw, we could see the flames rising from the ghetto at night. It took the Germans three weeks before they could enter the ghetto, and they still met some resistance. But after a while, those who had survived finally gave up.

Most were taken to Auschwitz. The Germans then believed that they had finished off the Polish Jews.

Meanwhile, outside of Poland, the situation became

more promising. We became more hopeful that we would survive this terrible war, which now had been going on for nearly four years. It was already spring and our farmer and his family were beginning to work in the fields.

We spent our time in the bunker discussing the possibility of survival and what the future might be in post-war Poland. Since most Poles helped the Germans with the destruction and elimination of the Jewish people, we all agreed that we could not stay.

If the opportunity arose, and we were lucky enough to survive, then we must leave Poland.

As the days turned into weeks and the weeks into months, we never gave up hope.

Then one day—it was a Sunday in June—our farmer came home from church and told us that we would have to leave for some other place. Apparently, at the church, a fellow who worked with the Germans, and had been given a rifle and other weapons, told him that some people in the village were saying that he was hiding Jews on his farm.

This was very bad news for us. We had no choice, even though we did not believe his story. Perhaps he was under great stress, since there was occasional news that the Germans had found Jews hiding on a farm and they would kill the farmer and his entire family. They would also burn the farm to the ground. We decided to leave. Perhaps after a while he would take us back.

We decided to go back to the barn we had stayed in

before. When we arrived there, we found that the son of the deceased farmer had already taken down the shack we had lived in to make room for a house he was planning to build, since he was getting married. We asked him if we could stay for a while and he showed us the barn, which was completely empty. There was no place to hide in case of danger.

While we were on this farm, we noticed a young boy of about fifteen or so, who was working there. After speaking to him, we learned that his father had worked for us about nine years earlier and he remembered us. He told us that there was a lot of heavy brush on his father's property and that we could hide there for awhile. He thought that if we remained in the brush all of the time, we would be safe. We decided that this was better than nothing, even though we would be outside and exposed to the elements. So that night we went to the brush.

One evening, as we were walking out of the brush, I was walking behind Nathan when he let go of a branch, which had sharp thorns on it, and it hit me in the right eye. We then went back to the barn, since we were soaked from a rain which had lasted for about twenty-four hours. We stayed in the barn for a few days, since no one was there.

When I finally walked out of the barn, after the rain had stopped, I noticed that the vision of my right eye was foggy. I was sure that I had lost the sight in that eye permanently. I could not go to see an eye doctor, or any other kind for that matter.

When Nathan and Mendel looked at my eye, they said it looked like a cataract. Later, we went back to the brush where we felt a little safer, but we were not very happy, living in these conditions. We had noticed that not far from the brush there was a large stack of rocks about ten feet high.

I got the idea that we could build a bunker with these rocks. We talked with the young boy and asked him if he could buy us some lumber, which we could use as protection against the rain.

After he got the lumber, we spent one night taking apart a portion of the rock pile, making enough room for the three of us. We camouflaged the top and entrance. At first, the boy had to cover the entrance for us from the outside, but later we learned to close it ourselves. In the bunker, we had to keep an eye on our bread, since small field mice also had their homes in the rock pile.

We lived in this rock bunker for about six weeks. Of course, when it was dark, we would take walks and sometimes get food and water. I had arguments with Nathan, since his cigarette smoke would escape our fortress and could give us away, if someone would come near. One evening, we met Mendel's daughters in the back of the barn. As we came out to meet with them, Nathan lit up a cigarette in spite of my protests.

Perhaps ten minutes later, two Polish boys appeared, one carrying a rifle. When they began talking to us, Mendel's daughters excused themselves and disappeared.

The boys said that we were lucky to still be alive almost one year after the liquidation, and still looking healthy.

At times while we were talking to them, and we would be walking at some distance from them, we would talk between us about taking them on and taking away the rifle. But we were not sure who they were, since at that time many boys from the underground carried weapons. So we decided not to attempt to disarm them.

They then told us they had to go and they said good night. We turned around and began walking away when all of a sudden we heard a shot. Nathan, who was right next to me, said he was hit and couldn't keep his balance. We were running by that time, and I grabbed Nathan by his hand and we continued to run. Mendel was to my left and turned to the left. I saw him fall after the second shot was fired. Nathan and I were still running, and they were after us.

Nathan could not run any longer, since he was bleeding and losing strength. He stopped and hid in the potato patch. I was the only one still running as another shot was fired from a short distance. I could hear the bullet whisk by my right ear. At that same moment, I fell down because I had stepped into a deep trench, which I could not see since it was quite dark.

As I fell, they must have thought that they had shot me, and they returned to where Nathan had been and took another shot at him. They apparently then ran out of bullets and had to reload.

At that point, I crawled away, going to an area with tall corn plants. For about an hour I laid there. We always knew where we were to meet after any emergency, but I decided not to go there that night. Instead, I went to the woods about two miles away, on a hill, where I fell asleep, since I was extremely tired. I knew this area quite well.

Of course, I thought that I was now alone and that I had lost Mendel and Nathan.

The next day I stayed where I was, since I could not travel by light in case I might be seen. I hid in heavy brush till that evening. Under the cover of darkness, I started walking to our meeting place, which was the Borucs' colony, hoping for some miracle. I remember that it was the 15th of August, 1943, and the moon was big and bright. It was the night of a total lunar eclipse, and as I walked the moon began to disappear, until it was completely in the earth's shadow.

BACK TO THE SAFETY OF THE BORUCS

"If you Bermans are still alive, it means God is with you."

—MRS. BORUC

When I got to the house and knocked on the door, Mrs. Boruc opened the door and when she saw me, she crossed her heart with disbelief in her eyes, that I was still alive. They took me right to the bunker where Nathan and Mendel had come the night before.

Then I learned what had happened and how my brothers had survived. Mendel had fallen, not because he had been shot, but because he could not run any further and he had tripped on something. After a short time, he picked himself up and went to the Borucs' place, by a different route.

Nathan, having lost quite a bit of blood after being shot, managed to arrive at the house a few hours after Mendel. One of the Borucs' sons had some experience in treating gunshot wounds and had taken a chicken feather, dipped in iodine, and pulled it through the bullet hole in Nathan's shoulder.

The bullet had gone only through flesh and exited the shoulder completely. They had all believed that since I did not return to the Borucs the same night, that I had most likely been killed.

Luckily, Nathan's wound did not get infected, and after a while it healed nicely. A few days later, Mendel's daughters came to see us and told us that they had recognized the boy with the rifle, but that they had panicked and ran away. For a time, the Borucs let us stay in the bunker.

There was more encouraging news on the war. The German army was retreating on all fronts. We heard that the Americans had landed on Italian soil and were moving toward Rome, and this was especially good news. On the Russian front, the Germans were also retreating. This gave us all hope that we might eventually survive this terrible war.

Meanwhile, we received news that my sister Fay and Frank would have to leave their hiding place, since the village they were in was being searched for Jews. One Jewish boy, who had been hiding in a barn, had panicked and tried to run into the woods and had been captured. The boy had come to visit Fay and Frank and knew their hiding place. There was a real danger that they would be exposed, so when we met at night, it was decided that they would come and stay in our bunker.

We told only the sons of the farmer, promising them extra money so they would not tell their parents. We assured them that Frank and Fay would not stay long. They brought enough food to the bunker for only three people, not all five of us, but we did the best we could.

It was October 1943, and the war situation looked more encouraging. The German army was being defeated on all fronts.

We, in the bunker, began discussing what it would be like if we actually survived. Could we stay and live in Poland when most of the Jewish population had been destroyed? I personally believed that we could not stay in Poland, and that if we had a chance to emigrate to another country, we should go.

Weeks, then months went by. Then it was winter again, and a full year had passed since we had jumped from the train which was headed for the death camp, Treblinka.

From time to time the farmer's sons would bring us

leaflets from the Polish underground. From their radios, they picked up the news from Great Britain about the war. At times they received instructions and locations of weapons which were dropped from American and British planes, secretly arranged by radio.

One evening, the farmer's younger son came near our bunker and had with him about a dozen automatic, English-made machine guns and a box of hand grenades. He told us to take them into our bunker. We complied with his request, and stored them there.

WHERE IS NEPHEW SAM?

Often we would wonder what had happened to (nephew) Sam, after he had jumped from the same cattle car as the rest of us. But he had jumped from the other side, which was in front of the car. We would also talk about our brother Symcha and his family, who had been sent to Siberia by the Russians.

NOTE: Nathan's nephew and soccer teammate, Sam, leapt out the other side of the train and wound up near the Russian border. He, along with Symcha and family, will eventually reunite with the family in Kaluszyn and eventually emigrate to the US.

Sam, like his relations, was a resolute survivor. He knew of a Polish girl named Stefa Koszka, whom he would later marry. She lived with her parents in the countryside near Trzymuzsko. He found his way to her; she hid him in their barn and snuck food to him. Sam was well-known for his tremendous appetite. In Kaluszyn, when asked what he would like to eat, he would often reply, "A kibel mit lokshen" or a barrel of noodles. Eventually, Stefa's parents noticed the missing food and Sam had to move on.

Sam then found his way into Russia and came across a unit of the underground, which he promptly joined. This group of Jewish and Russian partisans actively worked, disrupting and destroying train tracks and German supply lines. The following is a firsthand account of Sam's activity.

CHAPTER TWENTY-THREE

KALUSZYN PARTISANS

By the Brothers Shinolecki

"IN THE SUMMER OF 1942, JEWS FROM KALUSHIN were driven to Mrozi on the way to the death camps in Treblinka. We already knew at that time the meaning of Treblinka. We experienced many actions and developed a skill how to escape. From far we could hear the shots in Mrozi, as the Jews from Kalushin were forced into the death wagons on the way to Treblinka. In 1943, we were joined by two Jews that escaped Treblinka during a Jewish rebellion there. They did not stay long. One went with my brother Israel to bring some food; the Polish peasants handed them over to the police. We found them shot with their hands tied. The other escapee from Treblinka was shot by a Pole for refusing to let him extricate his golden tooth. The peasants told the Germans about our bunker in the woods; we escaped.

We retreated deep in the forest, and were witness to

the transportation of the last Jews from Kaluszyn. The Germans tricked them, promising food and resettlement. We did not believe the Germans.

In 1944, we settled in the region of Kupler forest, one day we left our bunker and noticed an armed German in our vicinity. We started to run, to our amazement we heard him call out to us in a familiar Yiddish. "Come here, I am a Jew from Kaluszyn." We asked him to put down his weapon, indeed he was Yeheshua (Sam) Berman clad in a German uniform. We found out that not far from us existed a strong group of Jewish and Russian partisans. We were hungry, we were emaciated, we did not have strength to carry our weapons.

That very night they collected us clothing, and thus began a new interesting and active life in a large group of partisans. We were assigned to plaster the railways with mines between the towns of Shedletz and Tzeglov. When we returned home to Kaluszyn, the local non-Jewish population "received" us by murdering our comrade Shmuel Lev, it became clear to us that we could not stay in Kaluszyn anymore."[5]

5   The Brothers Shinolentzky, *Partisans in the Kaluszyn Area*, translated by Gooter Goldberg, in "Sefer Kalushin" published by the Kalushiner Societies in Israel, the United States of America, Argentine, France and other countries (Tel-Aviv, 1961).

CHAPTER TWENTY-FOUR

AUTOBIOGRAPHY OF A SURVIVOR, PART IX

Kaluszyn, 1944—Joseph Berman

IT WAS ALREADY THE BEGINNING OF 1944 AND there were rumors that the Americans had landed on Italian shores and the battles on the other fronts were getting closer to us. From all this news we really began to believe that we had a chance to survive this terrible war.

But in February, we received some very bad news. The farmer and his family called us to their house one evening and told us that we would have to leave that night, since the gestapo had arrested a member of the underground and they were afraid that, under torture, he might tell where the weapons were hidden.

Since they were in our bunker, there was a risk that they would come to our bunker and find more than just the weapons. We had no choice but to leave. With nowhere else to go, we just left that night. The snow was at least three feet deep, and a blizzard with unbelievably strong winds was taking place. At least our tracks would be well covered.

There were five of us and the walking was very hard. After walking for about one and a half hours, we arrived at a small forest consisting of young pine trees, not taller than nine to ten feet. Since we were exhausted by that time, we decided to stay there.

With only some bread and water, we could only last there for about two or three days. We took short naps, alternating the person who had to stay awake and keep watch, and make sure we wouldn't freeze to death.

As the morning came, we noticed a windmill not too far away. This was the same mill I used to see from our backyard in Kaluszyn. We realized that we were only a few kilometers from our home. It was very cold, and we had nowhere to go for shelter. We even discussed the possibility of going back to Kaluszyn and sneaking into our factory, which was empty and from information we had received, was idle and locked up.

But after considering the dangers of returning, we decided to stay where we were for a few days. Frank started complaining that his right leg was in great pain, and we were out of bread and water.

We decided to go back to the other Borucs to discuss our current situation. That night the sky was clear, but we were not sure which direction we should go. We only knew that when we left the farm we had gone south, so we would have to go north.

I found the North Star, but when we began to travel, Frank could not walk on his ailing leg. He insisted that we leave him behind, but Nathan and I held him under his arms, which allowed him to walk only on his good leg. Despite the bitter cold, we were soaked with perspiration, walking in deep snow. We had to stay away from the roads so we would not be seen.

Finally, we arrived at the village of the Borucs. When we got to their home, they gave us some bread and hot soup. We could not stay there, however, due to the danger of being discovered. We had nowhere to go but back into the woods. We decided to stay closer to the village, in a portion of the forest we had hidden several months earlier.

Since it was too cold to survive at night, we snuck back to the farm that evening, and entered through the lower end of the roof, which was covered with only bunches of straw. The farmer's dog, which ran loose at night, recognized us and did not bark when we approached. So each night we would go back to the barn, where it was warmer and we could sleep without freezing to death.

One day we decided to go back to the people who had been hiding Frank and Fay, in hopes that they might agree to take them back, at least until the weather warmed up, since spring was not too far off. Also, we believed that the end of the war was near. After discussing our plight with those people, they agreed to take them in for a short time.

This was a great relief for us, since it was much easier for three to move around at night, to and from the barn, and to find food. Nathan, Mendel, and I had nowhere to go but to the forest during the day, and back to the barn each night.

And so it was till the end of the winter of 1943. We had managed to survive the greatest hardship so far, the extremely cold and bitter winter. We also realized that Frank and Fay would probably return soon and stay with us and that things would again become more difficult, as far as getting enough food and shelter.

It was early April, and as unlikely as a search of the farm became, farmer Boruc was not ready to let us come back. One evening, as we came to his farmhouse, he told us that Mendel's oldest daughter, who had been staying at his brother's house, was sick with some severe headaches. They could not get any medicine for pain for her.

We were still in the woods for many weeks after that, and one evening the farmer told us that we could stay for a short while and recuperate, but we would have to leave after a while. That was a pleasant surprise, and as long as things were quiet he did not tell us to leave.

One day, the younger son came to our bunker and called me and Nathan out, and told us that Mendel's oldest daughter had died that afternoon in his uncle's barn. He said that we would have to travel that night to get her body and arrange for burial.

This was the most painful day of my entire life, and I have no words to describe my feelings at that time.

The thought of telling Mendel about his daughter's death, and the task awaiting us was horrifying to me. And where to bury her? I had hoped that this night would never come. But nature ignores human feelings and goes ahead and does what nature is assigned to do.

The night came, and Nathan and I decided to let Mendel stay at the barn, because it would be too painful for him to cope with such an ordeal. The farmer's oldest son took two shovels and gave one to me and one to Nathan. We walked about two kilometers to a field along the road, where Boruc's brother was already waiting, with the body of Mendel's oldest daughter. He quickly left us, and returned to his village.

Without saying a word, we picked up the body on our shoulders and began walking, without knowing where we were going to stop. We finally decided to go to the nearest forest, which was about a mile away, and bury her there. When we returned, Mendel asked us only where we had laid her to rest.

In about the middle of May, 1944, Frank and Fay had to come back to our hiding place. We took them in, but without the permission of the farmer this time. A few weeks went by and we had to again leave the farm and return to the woods. Since it was quite a bit warmer now, we did not bother to return to the farm each evening. We only went back when we ran out of food and water. One night around midnight, we heard a plane circling above without any lights for about half an hour.

We were certain that it was British looking for a place to drop something. When the sun came up, we could hear machine gunfire in the distance. Somehow we were not too concerned, since we had heard gunfire many times before. But in about half an hour we suddenly realized that we could hear gunshots from both directions of our camouflaged hideout.

We then could hear the voices of German soldiers. Soon, we could see two of them, holding automatic rifles.

Whenever we left our bunker, I always took two hand grenades with me, in case we had to defend ourselves. I pulled out the safety pin and was prepared to toss it, but they passed us without incident. I put the pin back into the hand grenade. We learned later that the Germans were searching for whatever that plane had dropped the night before. They had suspected paratroopers or weapons might be in the area. The farmer and his wife and sons had watched the Germans walk into the woods where we were staying and were certain that we had been captured. Later, when they found out that they had missed us, they were amazed.

Three days later, while Frank was walking about fifteen feet from our hideout, a young boy from the nearest village saw him and said that Frank and the rest of us were lucky to have escaped the Germans who had been nearby three days ago.

When the boy returned to his village and told the villagers about us, they decided to call the Germans and tell them where we were. When they did, the Germans told them that they would come for us early the next morning. But the village leader had known about us, since he used to come to Kaluszyn and buy jackets from our family. He had to call the Germans in the presence of other villagers, but later called in his brother, whom he told to go to the woods and warn us. When it got dark, we heard someone heading toward our hiding place. Suddenly, a big man appeared in front of us.

He asked if we were the Bermans from Kaluszyn. When we told him we were, he introduced himself as the brother of the leader from the village. He then warned us to leave for a safer place since the Germans would be coming for us in the morning. We thanked him and he left.

A short time later, the weather became threatening and dark clouds covered the sky. Lightning and thunder were followed by a heavy rainstorm. We were grateful for this, however, since the Germans usually came with German Shepherds, and it would be difficult for them to follow our trail. We decided to go back to our farmer, in hopes that he would take us in again.

We were about three-quarters of a mile from the farm, but to cover our tracks, we went south instead of north and wound up traveling more than six miles, practically making a complete circle. It was pouring rain the entire time.

When we finally arrived at the farm, we were soaked

to the bone. We knocked on the door and asked if we could come in. When they saw us, they told us what had happened three days ago, and they were certain that we had been captured.

They really believed that God was with us...

We did not tell them why we had come to them on this night. We did not want them to know that the Germans would be searching for us the next morning. We asked them only if we could stay and rest for a few days. We could tell that they felt very sorry for us, and they agreed to take us in. Frank and Fay stayed out of sight, however, since we wanted them to think that there were only three of us who needed shelter.

They gave us some food and we went down to the bunker, taking Frank and Fay along, of course. We were very tired and fell asleep almost at once without saying a word to one another. We were awakened by the farmer, telling us that the woods we had just left the night before were surrounded by the Germans and police with their tracking dogs. He was worried that they would pick up our trail, but we told him not to worry since it had rained and we took such great pains to avoid leaving a trail to his farm. He relaxed after we explained this to him.

The Germans searched the woods for about one and one-half hours and then left. After they were gone, the farmer came close to the bunker and told us again that God must be with us, and from then on we could stay with him as long as necessary.

Meanwhile, the news about the war continued to be encouraging. On the Soviet front, the Red Army, according to underground reports, was nearing our area with unbelievable speed. And there were rumors that on the western front, the Americans and the Allies had landed in northern France, in a place called Normandy.

We later found out that it was true. It was early June of 1944. Our farmer was in very good spirits, realizing that the war might actually be coming to an end, and that they might really survive along with us.

The farmer's entire family began treating us better. They gave us more food, and everyone seemed happy.

One day the farmer's son returned from the village with a newspaper which proclaimed that Hitler would destroy everything on his retreat. And that no house or farm would escape, and everything would be burned to the ground. Everyone believed that he would carry out this threat. Since our bunker was attached to the outside of the barn, we knew that if the barn were set on fire, we would not survive, since we could not run away without being seen by the Germans.

We decided that we would talk to the farmer's sons about building another bunker, this time in the field, where the grain grew tall. After a while, they agreed.

One night the farmer's two sons, along with us, dug a large hole in the ground about one hundred meters from the existing bunker, and covered it with large boards and a camouflaged entrance. We finished it the very same night. Now we had a place to escape in case they started burning our area.

And sure enough, that new bunker, some two months later, saved our lives. Without it we would have certainly perished. The news about the war continued to be very encouraging. Germany was being bombed day and night by the Allies, crippling their war industry. American troops were making great progress on the western front in France. There were rumors that Paris had been liberated.

On the eastern front, the battles were already on Polish soil. All of Romania had been recaptured from the Germans. It was already July and some German army units, lost from their main command, were retreating through nearby villages. This we learned from passing farmers.

Good news was coming from every direction and we could feel, in the air, that freedom might be near. A few days later, there were reports that the Soviet army broke through a wide front, just south of us, perhaps only one hundred kilometers away, and that the Germans were retreating north, toward us. Every hour we heard more news that the German army was backing up north, since the Soviets cut off the main road running from Lublin to Warsaw.

One night, near the end of July, a tremendous noise woke us and lasted for a few days. We learned that a large German motorized unit was attempting to avoid being totally surrounded by the Soviet army. They chose a side road which ran parallel to the main road to Warsaw and Siedlec, and that road was only about one kilometer from our farm.

On the second day, a battle erupted between German and Russian tanks, right in front of our farm, only about one-half kilometer away. We could hear the explosions from artillery shells above us.

The next day we found out that the Germans set up a command post on our farm, and took it over to plan their defense. Because the farm was far from the village, they could work without being detected.

They let the farmer and his wife stay, so they could feed and take care of the needs of the Germans. They were allowed to take care of their cows, pigs, and horses. When the farmer's wife went to feed the pigs, which were close to our bunker, she pretended to be talking to herself, knowing that we would hear her. In this way, she informed us that the Germans were occupying the farmhouse. Fortunately, we had some food in the bunker. Enough to last a day or so.

We knew that freedom was near, and yet, so far away.

That same afternoon it started to rain. This was good, since we knew that the Germans would stay inside most of the time. We hoped that they would leave soon. It rained for a few days, without stopping. All of a sudden our bunker began to fill up with rainwater.

We had no way to stop it. In a short time, we were sitting with water up to our chests. We sat in the bunker, filled with water for twenty-four hours, and the rain still continued. We felt that we were getting weaker with every passing hour. All of our clothes were rotting, and they were the only clothes we had.

We decided to leave the bunker that night and get into the barn from the back, so no one could see or hear us. To our surprise, when we got out of the bunker, none of us could stand up. We had spent so much time in the water, that we were extremely weak.

We had to crawl on our hands and knees, but we made it. In the barn was freshly cut clover, so we covered ourselves with it and were able to hide. It also allowed us to dry ourselves off.

We then decided to go to the bunker in the fields. When night came we still could not walk, since our legs could not yet support the weight of our bodies. We crawled into the bunker and covered the entrance with freshly harvested straw from the fields. It made a perfect camouflaged entrance.

In the morning, we could still hear the sounds of artillery fire for a period of time. After a while, however, it ceased. For food, we pulled straws from our entrance and took out the rye seeds and ate them for several days.

LIBERATION BY THE SOVIETS

On the morning of August 9, 1944, we heard footsteps coming toward our bunker, then the voice of the farmer's wife. She told us that the Germans had left the night before, and that some Russian soldiers had already arrived in the village. We were finally free to come out of our hiding place.

We could not move. We could not believe that we were finally free to come out. As we came out, she was surprised to see Frank and Fay. She asked us who they were, and how they got here. We, of course, told her that they had arrived just a few days ago.

Most of us did not have shoes, due to the water we were sitting in for several days. It caused the soles to come unglued. We could already stand on our feet, but had difficulty walking in the fields, since they had been recently harvested and the remaining stalks were quite sharp. We discovered, however, that by sliding our feet, rather than walking, we could get around without too much discomfort.

We came into the farmer's house and had something to eat. The farmer asked us to promise not to tell anyone that he had allowed us to stay with him. This we did. We went back to the barn and laid down for awhile. We discussed the possibility of a German counterattack, which would place us back in the same situation we were in the day before. We seriously considered traveling east for a few hundred kilometers, to the eastern part of Poland. But since we had no shoes or clothes, we decided to stay and take our chances.

The next day, a Jewish Soviet officer came to the farm

and took up temporary residence there. We identified ourselves to him as fellow Jews, and asked him of the possibility that the Germans might come back, and whether he thought we should travel east. He took out a bulletin, written in Russian, and told us that the Red Army had already taken Prague, which is on the very outskirts of Warsaw.

On the other fronts, the Soviet army had moved much farther into Poland. On the western front, the Allies were making great progress and there was already fighting in Belgium. He did not believe that the Germans would be in a position to go on the offensive at that time, since they were being pushed back on almost every front.

After hearing this, we decided to return to Kaluszyn, which was only about eight kilometers southwest of the farm. Most of us were barefoot, but I decided to carry the remaining upper part of my boots, since they were still in good condition.

As we walked toward the woods, where we had hidden most of the time, we were stopped by some Soviet soldiers and were asked who we were and where we were going. We told them our story. They had already known what had happened to the Jews and let us go. When we passed through their lines, we could see their anti-tank guns and heavy rocket launchers.

A Soviet driver saw us walking barefoot and asked us where we were headed. We told him that we were traveling to Kaluszyn and he told us that he was going in that direction and offered us a ride in his truck. We gladly accepted his offer and hopped on the truck, which was loaded with boxes of ammunition.

Fifteen minutes later we were on the outskirts of Kaluszyn. He let us off outside of the city.

As we started to walk toward the city, we ran into several people who recognized us. They could not believe that we had survived the Holocaust. They had seen us being taken away by the Germans some twenty months earlier, with all the other Jews in the town. And here we were, as though from another world.

They asked us where we had been, and how it was possible that we managed to escape. We headed to our homes, only to find that the Russians had been in Kaluszyn for a week and some of their units were lodged in some of our houses. They had been vacated by several Polish families who had left for the country before the battle for the city began. So the houses had been left quite empty, except for some temporary bunks made of lumber and straw.

IN KALUSZYN, ONLY ABOUT 10 TOTAL JEWISH SURVIVORS OUT OF 8,000 BEFORE THE WAR

NOTE: Of these ten, five were members of the Berman family who survived in the Kaluszyn countryside. Both of Mendel's daughters perished from typhus.

- Nathan
- Mendel
- Joseph
- Fay (sister)
- Frank (brother-in-law)

Six more family members would soon join them after surviving the war in Russia and undergoing their own harrowing escapes.

We moved into one of our homes, which was still vacant. Some of our neighbors came in to greet us and offered help. The city priest heard that some of the Bermans had returned, and brought us some food, and seemed happy to see us.

One boy, who had served with me in the same regiment of the Polish army, saw that I was barefoot, and since he was a shoemaker, offered to repair my boots. He did so almost immediately. Several merchants who had known us, gave us shirts, on credit, since we had no money at that time.

Farmers from around Kaluszyn heard that some of the Bermans had survived and began bringing us raw sheepskins, which they had accumulated during the war, to be tanned and made into coats for them.

And so, in this way we began to earn some money in order to support ourselves.

But the war was still not far from us. The German army was still in Warsaw, only fifty kilometers away.

We were still concerned that they might master a counteroffensive, and again overrun our area, putting us in the same mess as before. We discussed the possibility of evacuating and going farther east, but without any Jews left in the neighboring cities and towns to the east, we would not get any help with food, shelter, and other necessities.

So, we decided to stay in Kaluszyn and take our chances, hoping that the Germans would be unable to mount any offensive action. We felt that they would have to transfer many of their troops to the western front to meet the American, British, and French forces, which were already nearing German territory.

Meanwhile, the new Polish Communist government, formed by the Soviets, began calling up all young men, by the year of their birth for physicals, to be drafted into the Polish army and help fight the Germans. Although Frank and I were given physicals, and passed, we were never called for duty.

We were getting more and more business from people in the city, as well as farmers, since our reputation for quality work had been well-known throughout the area for many years.

Meanwhile, Sam arrived and told us that he had been liberated three weeks before us. Since he was involved with the Russian partisans, the Soviet army enlisted his entire unit to the Soviet reserves and sent them to Russia for training.

But Sam left the train, at one of its stops, and purposely returned late, after it had already left the station. He later asked the local police for the location of the Polish Embassy in Moscow, and they escorted him there. There he met a Polish officer who, after questioning Sam, found out he was from Kaluszyn. He was familiar with the town and tested Sam by asking him the names of some of his friends.

Luckily, he recognized some of the names and realized that Sam was telling him the truth. At that time, everyone was suspected as a possible enemy of the Soviet Union.

After Sam convinced the officer that he was truly a Polish citizen, and from Kaluszyn, he gave him a certificate to travel back home by train. During his train ride back home, Sam decided to stop off at the village where Stefa lived. There he met some men from Kaluszyn who told him that some members of the Berman family had survived and had returned to Kaluszyn. He made his visit to Stefa a short one and rushed home to see who was alive.

No one can describe the moment of the meeting between Sam and the rest of us who had survived. We hadn't seen each other since we had jumped from the train, which was taking us to the death camp at Treblinka. It had been twenty months, and we did not know Sam's fate, and he did not know ours.

Now there were seven of us. Some other young Jews had survived in the woods and had heard about us. They came to see us, and we took them in and gave them food and shelter. We treated them as though they were family.

One day, two Russians dressed in army uniforms came into our house and began asking us how we had survived. They told us they were news reporters for the Russian newspapers and would help us to get things we needed if we just told them about our experiences during Hitler's campaign of genocide against the Jews. They told us that they were very busy at that moment, but they would let us know when we should come to their offices.

One morning, some time afterward, a courier arrived and asked us to go with him to the reporters' offices. When we arrived, we were surprised to see that they were using one of our cousin's homes as their offices. They served us tea and began asking us about our experiences during the German occupation.

They seemed interested in which of the Polish people in the area had collaborated with the Germans, against the Jews. We soon realized that they were attempting to obtain from us the names of members of the Polish underground. But we told them that since we were away from Kaluszyn for nearly two years, we were unaware of any people who had belonged to the so-called A.K.

This type of questioning went on for a few days. Finally, they realized that they were not going to get any information from us, and stopped asking us to come back.

One day a couple named Schmuel and Hadassah Lev arrived in town. She was a distant relative of ours. They had survived the war in the eastern part of Poland, which had been controlled by the Russians, until the Germans attacked in June of 1941. This was the territory that Hitler had given to Stalin before the war so that the Russians would not enter the war against Germany. They had managed to survive in the woods, in much the same way as we had.

Before the war, Schmuel Lev had belonged to the Communist party in Poland, which had been outlawed. He had served a jail sentence for Communist activities. So, it was only natural for him to go to Soviet-controlled territory when the war broke out. We were never too close to them, since before the war we were considered capitalists in Kaluszyn. When he was released from jail, he married Hadassah.

A few days after Lev arrived, he joined with other Polish Communists with the ambition of becoming the government leaders of the city of Kaluszyn, with the help of the Russian military authorities. And so it was; he and his Polish friends from the party became the most trusted group in the city by the Soviet secret service.

We were told that at one meeting Lev criticized the wealthier people in the town, including us, for not abandoning our capitalistic dreams. Soon, after his wife became pregnant, he moved into a larger apartment. He also received a permit to carry a gun, for his protection, and soon became the "king" of the town.

After a month or two, Nathan went to the neighboring town of Wengrow to see who had survived there. In Wengrow, he met Mira. When he returned, he told us of a family he had met by the name of Prepurka. They had survived the war in nearly the same way as we had. There were three brothers and two sisters and a brother-in-law. They had been in the leather business before the war, selling leather for shoe soles in Warsaw, not far from where we had our store.

A few days later, they came to Kaluszyn to see us. When they saw our facilities, and our factory, they proposed to us that we form a partnership and manufacture shoe sole leather parts, since they were quite experienced in the process.

With our factory by the creek, they felt that it would be the perfect place to operate such a business. We agreed, and started the operation almost immediately. One of them came to live with us.

One day, Mira came to town to meet the rest of us. She stayed a few days, and after awhile, she and Nathan decided to get married. The wedding took place in our house, without a rabbi being present.

NOTE: There were no rabbis left in Kaluszyn at this time. The head Russian officer conducted a civil ceremony.

Mira Rotstein, Front row seated
(From top left to right) Maria, Renie Schinary, Annie Wengrowie, Poland, 1942

Mira's story of survival was equally as harrowing. She was born in the small village of Wolomien. Her parents were brutally murdered by the Germans. Then fifteen years old, Mira and her brother, Gershon, escaped to the countryside. She was able to obtain a fake Polish I.D. that identified her as a young orphaned Polish girl named Yanina Yablinski. She was brought up going to public schools and spoke only Polish. Mira was able to procure a position as a housekeeper for a Polish couple. Shortly after she began work, the woman who employed her became aware of Mira's exceptional ability as a knitter of sweaters, socks, hats, and mittens. She was very comfortable in her position with the family. However, the husband of the house was working with the Germans, actively rounding up renegade Jews and turning them over to the Germans for a bounty. One day as she went out to do her chores, she came across a young Jewish boy tied up in the barn. She quickly realized that the boy recognized her and knew she was also Jewish. Fearing that during interrogation the young boy would expose her, Mira knew she would have to leave. As the sun set and darkness prevailed, she made her escape into the woods. After a few days had passed, and realizing that her employer's husband and young Jewish boy were no longer at the home, she returned to the house and pleaded with the woman to give her back her I.D. The woman retrieved Mira's documents and told her to leave before her husband returned.

Meanwhile, the Soviet army began its winter offensive against the Germans, and a large part of Western Poland was freed from occupation, including Warsaw and Lodz.

Near the end of September, 1944, my brother Mendel's younger daughter, Mania, began having severe headaches. These were similar to the symptoms her older sister had just before she died four months earlier, while in hiding.

We took her to the hospital in Minsk, a neighboring city of Kaluszyn. After six days there, she also died. Again, Mendel and I took a horse and buggy to pick up the body of one of his daughters. It is hard to describe my feelings at that time. It took us about six hours both ways, to the hospital and then back to the cemetery.

We did not speak a single word. When we arrived at the cemetery, there were no gravestones or monuments anywhere. Nor was there anyone who could perform a service, or help us in the burial. We had to do it all ourselves.

It was now the winter of 1944 to 1945, and the Soviet troops stationed in our area were getting new sheepskin coats for the winter. They sold these coats to the population in order to buy food and vodka.

But people were afraid to wear these coats as they were, and brought them to us for restyling and color changes. As a result, we began running out of dyes used for coloring. Sam and I decided to travel to the city of Siedlec, which had survived the war and had not been destroyed.

The only way to get there, however, was by Soviet army truck. The drivers would carry passengers and receive payment in the form of vodka, or other desirable goods. So, we went out to the main road which ran between Warsaw and Moscow. One of the Soviet trucks stopped and gave us a ride to Siedlec. When we arrived, we went to the city hall and asked where we could find dye and other products we needed to color leather or sheepskin.

After we found the items we needed, we decided to meet with some other local Jewish survivors. Sam had met a young woman named Chipa, who had been hidden by Stefa's parents as he had been. She had a little girl, about nine years old. This woman had lived, before the war, not far from Stefa's village and she had known her parents for some time.

Since we had waited for quite some time for a truck which could return us home, and none came, we decided to walk with Chipa to her village. It was about eighteen kilometers from where we were. As we neared the outskirts of the village, Chipa pointed out a house where a Jewish girl had lived with a Polish woman. The Polish woman did not know that the girl was Jewish. She sold kielbasa, and I wanted to go over and buy some. But Chipa said that I should not, since the Jewish girl did not want to be identified at that time. She was afraid that if her religion were discovered, she might be killed. So, I did not go over to that house.

When we arrived at Chipa's house, we met a Jewish girl named Jadzia, who had also survived in the same house as Sam and Chipa. She told us that the next night was going to be Christmas Eve. We all decided to go to the next village where Stefa's parents lived and help them celebrate the holidays. I went along with them and met Stefa and her family for the first time. We stayed there for two nights and then we returned home. Stefa decided to come along with us.

It was a few days before New Year's 1945, about five months after we had been liberated. The city hall organized a New Year's Eve party, and we were invited. There we met many people we had known for years; of course all of them were gentiles.

There were only about ten Jews left who had survived in our town, out of approximately 8,000 before the war. Some of the Polish people were genuinely friendly, but most pretended. But we had a good time at the first New Year's celebration we had in many years.

During this time we were getting along fairly well financially, and had enough money to buy food and clothing. We were also able to save some money which we exchanged for US dollars. This was necessary since the new Polish government kept changing their paper currency into new ones frequently, and every time you exchanged your old money for the new, you got less.

At times we would hear that Jewish survivors, in some places, were being murdered by the Poles with excuses like they had collaborated with the Soviet KGB against the Polish underground. We also heard that former criminals had formed gangs and had obtained quite a few weapons during the retreat of the German army; during the night they would break into the homes of those with some money or other wealth, rob them of their valuables, and murder the entire household.

We had a few sawed-off rifles ourselves, which we had obtained from three Jewish brothers who had survived in the forest, not far from where Sam had been hiding. When the Germans had left our area, the brothers had come to stay with us for awhile and had left the rifles and ammunition in our possession.

During the months of January and February, 1945, we barricaded ourselves at night by securing the doors and windows, against a possible break-in. There were occasions when someone would knock at our door late at night and tell us they were the police. We would tell them to come back in the morning and they would leave. After these occurrences, we decided to move to the city of Lodz, where most of the Jewish survivors were then concentrated. Everyone in our family, except Sam and I, left Kaluszyn to look for a place to live in Lodz.

One morning, two boys from the underground went to Schmuel Lev's house. There they shot and killed Schmuel and another Jewish young man. They did not, however, harm his wife or child. Sam and I were preparing to leave at that point. We hired a Pole who had a horse and buggy, and loaded everything we could in it. We gave him an address in Warsaw-Praga, where he was to unload everything. It was the apartment of a friend.

Sam and I stayed in Kaluszyn for a few days, but at night we pretended to leave town by taking a Soviet truck, which was heading toward Warsaw. But after he traveled a few kilometers, we would get off the truck and go to a farmer who knew us well, and was from a very fine family, and spend the night with him. The next morning we would come back to Kaluszyn, from the same direction we had left the evening before.

We finally made our decision to leave Kaluszyn once and for all the very next day. It had become too dangerous.

CHAPTER TWENTY-FIVE

AUTOBIOGRAPHY OF A SURVIVOR, PART X

New Worlds, New Lives—Joseph Berman

SAM TOOK A TRUCK WHICH WAS HEADING EAST, going to Stefa's village, and I took a truck which was heading west, to the neighboring city of Minsk, where two Jewish sisters had survived and lived. I stayed there overnight.

The next morning, I took a truck going to Praga, which was a suburb of Warsaw, where the Pole had delivered some of our merchandise several days earlier.

When I arrived, I met a girl named Pola who had come from Kaluszyn who was living with a sister, Hanka, and their uncle Kiva. They told me that they already had an apartment in Lodz and that we should go there as soon as possible.

After a few days, Nathan had come from Lodz and

we were preparing to go there with him and take everything with us. We first packed the skins, which were ready for manufacturing into garments. They fit into two large burlap bags.

We hired a man with a horse and buggy, who was supposed to take us to the main railroad station in Warsaw. From there we planned to take the train which went to Lodz. But when we arrived at the bridge which crosses the Vistula River, we saw that it had been destroyed.

We learned that it had been the work of the retreating German soldiers. They had also destroyed the other bridges leading to Warsaw.

We had to unload the sacks of skins and paid the driver. We learned from people in the area that we could hire a small boat to take us to the other side, which was to return in about half an hour. The Vistula was about one and a half times the width of the Detroit River. When we finally got to the other side, we were shocked by the sight of the almost total destruction of the city of Warsaw.

We saw only a few people walking around. We could not find any sort of transportation we could take with our goods to the railroad station. We knew that we were only about one-half kilometer from the station at that point, and decided to carry the sacks on our backs for that relatively short distance.

When we finally arrived, we were shocked to find the railroad station and all the tracks completely destroyed. We had no choice, at this point, but to carry the sacks on our backs again for a distance of about six or seven kilometers to where the western railroad station was located. We were told that that station had already been repaired and was in operation.

As we walked, we could not believe the extent of the devastation of Warsaw. On street after street, every building laid in ruins. Nothing but rubble for miles. From time to time, we would see people searching through the ruins, looking for some personal belongings which may have survived the devastation.

When we saw people, we would stop and ask them if they knew when the train for Lodz might be leaving, and how much farther the station was. Some told us that a train for Lodz would leave twice a day, once in the morning and once at sunset. If we hurried, we might make the evening train. We did not want to spend the night in Warsaw, so we began to hurry as fast as we could.

Even though we were hungry, we did not stop. After a few more hours, we finally arrived at the train station, and we were not too late. The train was at the station. We bought our tickets and boarded the train. We still had time, so we bought some food and had a chance to sit down and relax, at last.

The trip to Lodz took about twelve hours. When we arrived, we hired a horse and buggy to drive the few kilometers to our new apartment. I had never seen the apartment before, and was somewhat surprised to learn that we were on the fourth floor, and there was no elevator. We had to carry all those heavy sacks on our backs, all four flights.

When I had only about two steps left to reach the fourth floor, I felt some sort of click below my right knee. At first I didn't feel any pain, but after a couple hours I began to experience severe pain in my lower back, which went all the way down to my ankle. With each passing hour, the pain became more unbearable. Within a few days, I was totally crippled, unable to take a single step, or even stand up.

I was not able to see a doctor for a few weeks. When I finally did, he prescribed twenty electrical treatments. After about twelve of those treatments, I started to feel an itch on the inside of my right leg. I began improving and was finally able to get around with the use of a cane. I continued to have severe pain, however.

One day, a friend of Sam's, who was staying with Stefa, came to our apartment to see me. He told me about the Jewish girl who had survived in the village where Chipa had lived. She had come to Lodz with some other Jewish girls from the city of Siedlec, and was staying in Chipa's apartment. He thought I should meet her.

A few days later, Nathan and I were invited to Chipa's apartment. I finally had the chance to meet this girl. Her name was Rena Cedrowicz, and I liked her right away. I invited her to go with me to see the Moscow Philharmonic Orchestra, which was playing in Lodz. That was around the end of April, or early May of 1945. After that evening, we began seeing each other practically every day.

Economically, things in Lodz were not so good. No one was buying sheepskin coats in the spring or summer, so we decided to branch out. Frank took a partner and went to the so-called "green market," and they bought and resold clothing, mostly brought in from East Germany. Nathan traveled to East Germany with the Kishels, to buy any kind of used cloth and other goods for resale in Lodz.

Sam, Mendel, and I were getting ready for the coming fall season by building up an inventory of sheepskin jackets, to be ready when the cold weather would begin around October. Sometime in May, Sam and Stefa were married. After the defeat of Germany and the end of the war, the Polish Jews who had survived in Russia began returning to their towns and villages.

We received a letter from my brother Symcha, that he, his family, and Chaim had left Siberian territory and were in southern Ukraine. He told us that his wife, Ethel, had given birth to a baby girl some six months earlier and they had named her Sarah, after our mother. We tried to reach him by telephone, but without success. Mail took about three months to arrive after being sent from people in Russia.

We had hoped that Symcha and his family would return soon from Russia, so that we could be together again after being separated for six years. The city of Lodz had become the most populated city in Poland after Warsaw had been destroyed. It became very crowded because most of the survivors from the concentration camps in Germany, as well as Polish Jews returning from Russia, settled there.

Financially, things were improving for us. We were even saving money, which we converted into US dollars. The Polish currency at that time, called zloty, was not at all stable because of constant changing of the bank notes, and a resulting decrease in value.

A few months had passed since I had met Rena, and it seemed that we liked each other very much. Soon we started talking about getting married. One day my brother Mendel had visited one of the locations where survivors from the concentration camps would gather to attempt to locate relatives. There, one of the committee members suggested that whoever had room in their apartment, should take in one or more of the returnees from the German camps. Edzia was one of those survivors, and Mendel brought her home to stay with us. Eventually, they decided to get married.

Nathan was spending most of his time in East Germany with Arthur Kishel, buying all kinds of merchandise to be sold in the Polish market. Since the end of the war, everything was in short supply. Meanwhile, the Polish police formed their own corrupt circle. They would frequently come to someone's apartment in the evening and search for "illegal" items, like gold or foreign propaganda, and wound up taking whatever they wished. And there was no one you could complain to. At times you could hear gunfire in the streets, and someone would be killed, with no explanation as to what had happened or why.

One day, Sam sent Kiva (Hanka's uncle) to sell an overcoat which Nathan had purchased in East Germany, at the marketplace. He was arrested by the police. They claimed that the coat had belonged to one of the police officers, and that it had been stolen a few days earlier. Of course, the other policemen were witnesses to this lie. Sam was put in jail and was very badly beaten. He was released only after we paid a few hundred thousand zlotys to the same corrupt policeman. It was almost anarchy, and no one could complain.

It was around September 1945, while Nathan was away that we began thinking that this was no place to stay and live. Some Jews had already begun to leave Poland for the American zone in West Germany. We also started to make plans to leave, but not until around the end of the year, so we could sell all of the sheepskin coats we had produced for the winter season.

In the meantime, Rena and I decided to get married. The woman who Rena was staying with, Chipa, thought that we should get married immediately, but I insisted that we wait till Nathan returned from East Germany. When Nathan finally came back, the wedding plans were made, and we were married on Sunday, November 17, 1945 in Lodz. The ceremony was conducted by an Orthodox Jew who wrote the entire marriage contract on a single sheet of paper, which we managed to lose within a short period of time. We lived together with the entire family.

Sam and Stefa shared an apartment with Arthur Kishel and his wife. In the middle of December, the Kishels, together with Frank and Fay, were the first to leave Poland for West Germany. Rena and I moved in with Sam and Stefa after the Kishels left.

Finally, on December 30, 1945 Rena and I began our journey to West Germany. We knew that the police were always at the railroad station, searching every Jew leaving the city of Lodz, and taking their money and valuables. We decided that rather than going to the western railroad station, from which you would normally head for Germany, we would go to the eastern station, to Warsaw and other destinations east. The police were not patrolling the eastern station.

So we bought tickets for Warsaw. When we arrived there, we bought tickets for Stetim, a former German city which was now part of Poland, as a result of the surrender of Germany. This city was on the Polish side of the border with East Germany. Since Rena did not look Jewish, she carried all of our money and other valuables on the train. We even sat separately, pretending we did not know each other. We were on the train for about sixteen hours, stopping in almost every town on the way.

When we arrived in Stetim, we already knew where we were to go. We had prearranged our destination with the people who had organized the crossing of the Polish and East German border. This was going to be accomplished by us getting a ride on a Soviet truck.

In the meantime, we had to spend the day in an upstairs flat. We met with the people who had made the arrangements and paid them for the trip to East Germany. It was about 10:30 p.m. and we, together with some other people, went downstairs and walked for a few blocks to a fenced-in area. The truck was already there, and had many people in it. Among them were many German families who had been displaced by the new Polish government, which had decided to give their property to Poles who had been made homeless during the war. It was so crowded on the truck that we had to stand. The truck was covered with canvas, so that we could not be seen from the outside.

When the truck reached the border, the driver ordered everyone to lay down. It was extremely cramped and Rena was kicked in the face by someone and her nose began bleeding heavily. At that point, we were at the guard station and had to remain silent. We heard the driver talking to the border guards, and it appeared that he already had made a deal with them. After a short time, the truck began to move and we were relieved when we realized we were in East German territory.

It was exactly midnight when we arrived in East Berlin. The driver stopped the truck and ordered everyone to get out. He told us to start knocking on doors of nearby homes, since there was a dusk-to-dawn curfew.

So, we started knocking on doors at random. Not knowing who lived there or how they would react once they opened their door. When someone opened the door in the first home we approached, we explained where we were coming from and that we needed a place to stay, at least until the morning. We were fortunate, they let us in.

As we walked in, we saw a high-ranking Soviet officer sitting in the room we had entered. For a moment we were frightened. But after telling him that we were Jewish and running away from Poland, he identified himself as a Jew as well. We began telling him the story of how we had survived the German occupation. I began to feel at ease with him and told him that our destination was the American zone in Berlin, and that we were going to meet my sister and brother-in-law there. He told us to take the subway the following morning to the Western sector, and he told us where to get on and where to get off.

The people who lived in the home gave us a room to sleep in for the night. We got up early the next morning and went to the subway station. We blended in with all the other people there, trying to act normally. Once we arrived at our destination, we were relieved to realize that we were actually in the Western zone of Berlin, controlled by the Allies. We asked people for directions, since we already had the address of the place we were to stay.

Some even offered to go with us, and show us exactly where we were headed. When we arrived, we met Michael Kishel. He showed us to our room, and it was extremely comfortable, much nicer than we had expected. He told us that Fay and Frank and his brother, Arthur, had already left Berlin for the city of Landshut, located near Munich in what was now being called West Germany.

To get to that area from Berlin, however, it was necessary to travel through Soviet-controlled territory. In Landshut, Henry Popowski and Henry Obron, who had survived the Mathausen Concentration Camp in Austria, had several apartments at their disposal. Any displaced Jews who wanted a place to stay in Landshut, were allowed to stay in those apartments.

We decided to stay in Berlin for the time being, however. At least until the rest of our family arrived from Poland. We were still waiting for Nathan and Mira, Sam and Stefa, and Mendel and Edzia to show up. We were also going to meet the two Kornblum sisters, who were survivors from Kaluszyn, and had stayed with us after the liberation.

Shortly after we arrived, Michael Kishel decided to leave Berlin in order to join his brother and wife. By this time, we had the entire apartment to ourselves. We felt safe and quite secure in the American zone of Berlin. For food, we were helped by the United Nations Relief Organization for displaced people. We also would receive our share of cigarettes, which were in very short supply in Germany at that time. Since neither of us smoked, we would sell them to Germans for good money, which we would use to buy those items which we needed.

About one week later, the rest of the family arrived in Berlin. Meanwhile, the Jewish Congress announced that any Jews who wanted to get assistance to emigrate from Germany would have to move into a temporary camp, called Schlachtensea Camp for Refugees. We all decided to move into the camp, with the hope of someday going to the United States.

Life in the camp was like being in the army. Everyone had duties to be performed. One day, not too long afterward, Rena complained that she did not feel well. She went to a German doctor. A few days later, he told us that Rena was pregnant. It was the end of February, 1946. We were getting messages from Fay and Frank that we should go to Landshut and join them there. They said we could get an apartment and they already had one. But we had to wait for legal transportation, since we did not want to take the risk of being caught in Russian-controlled territory. If we were, we could have been turned over to the Polish authorities and possibly be sent back to Poland.

So we waited for the opportunity to find legal transportation for the American zone of West Germany. One day, there was an announcement that only women could travel to West Germany. So Rena, Mira, Stefa, and the Kornblum sisters got together and decided that they should go to Landshut, with the expectation of finding better living conditions.

We packed whatever belongings they had and one day soon thereafter, several US Army trucks arrived in camp and most of the women left. Edzia, however, decided that she would not leave without Mendel, and remained behind with the rest of us. This was sometime in the end of February, or early March, 1946.

One month later, we received word from the American authorities that anyone who remained in the camp would be given permission to go to West Germany. So we began to pack our belongings, and finally left Berlin for good.

While the men were still in Berlin, a group from the Jewish organization, Haijas, came to Landshut to take applications for emigration to the United States. Since the husbands were still in Berlin, the wives had to complete the applications for both. Since none of them knew our birthdays, they had to make them up. That is the reason that, to this day, we all have incorrect birth dates on our legal papers.

While we were staying in Landshut, we learned from others arriving from Poland that my brother Symcha and his family, and Chaim, had arrived from Russia and were living in Lodz. We hired a man who traveled to Poland every few days to help bring Symcha and his family to Landshut.

After a few weeks, they arrived along with their little baby girl, Sara, who had been born in the Ukraine two years earlier. Symcha's two sons, Alter, who was seventeen years old, and Sam, age fifteen came as well.

At about the same period of time, we heard that in the

city of Kelce in Poland, there was a pogrom against the Jews which had resulted in the murder of forty-six young men and women, killed by Polish youths.

This resulted in a massive exodus of almost all of the Jews still remaining in Poland.

Hundreds of Jews, young and old, began to arrive in Landshut. There was not enough housing for them, so the American military authorities set up camps of tents on the outskirts of the city.

From time to time we would visit the camps with the hope of finding some relative or friend we had known, who might have survived. One day, Rena and I were walking through the camp, when Rena suddenly screamed out "Chajale," and she began hugging someone. Rena had recognized her cousin, since she had been a grown woman when they last met in 1940. But Chajale, or Helen, did not recognize her right away, since Rena had been a young girl at the time. Helen had been married in 1939, a few months before the war had started, but her husband had been killed in the Holocaust.

Helen stayed with us for only a few days. And when the group she had come to Germany with, another Zionist organization, decided to leave Landshut, she left also, with the hope of going to Palestine. The group temporarily settled in the British-controlled zone in West Germany.

SYMCHA'S SONS' PERILOUS JOURNEY TO PALESTINE

My brother Symcha's two sons, Alter and Sam, stayed in Landshut only a few months. They were members of a Zionist youth organization, which as its goal, was to bring all its members to Palestine. They went to a city in Germany called Griefenberg. There they were trained to farm. A few months later, the entire group was smuggled into Italy and later to France. From there they boarded a large French fishing boat, with a Greek crew. Their destination was Palestine.

As they approached the shores near Tel Aviv, British naval cruisers encircled their boat. The Greek crew abandoned ship and left the passengers to fend for themselves. The British towed the fishing boat to the island of Cyprus.

During this time, we learned that Mira, Stefa, and Fay were pregnant, in addition to Rena. On September 28, 1946, Rena gave birth to a baby boy. We named him Alter Pinchas, my father's Hebrew name. In February 1947, Mira gave birth to a son, Jakov. In March, Stefa had a girl, Nora. In April, Fay gave birth to a son, Isaac. In October 1947, Edzia and Mendel had a boy who they named Abraham.

As time passed in Landshut, we began to recuperate from the effects of the war, both emotionally and physically. We all found apartments to live in, and were being helped with food and other necessities by the United Nations Relief Organization for Refugees.

The Jewish community in Landshut continued to

grow as more survivors kept arriving, and settled there temporarily. A Jewish committee was formed to represent us in matters with the city authorities. By this time, there were fifty-five to sixty Jews living in Landshut.

Symcha received a letter from his sons in Cyprus, stating that they had already been there a few months and did not know when they would be allowed to leave. During 1947, some of the Jewish refugees finally begin emigrating from Germany. The Kishel brothers were the first to be called by the US Consulate. Others left for Australia, South America, and Canada. Our entire family had been registered to go to America, but our first choice was to settle in Palestine. Sam and Stefa, however, had decided to go to the United States.

Symcha later received a letter from his son, Sam, stating that he had finally arrived in Palestine. The British had agreed to allow those sixteen years and younger to enter the country. Alter, the older son, had to stay in Cyprus, however. Meanwhile, the United Nations began debate on the establishment of a Jewish homeland in a portion of Palestine.

There were fears that if the United Nations granted a new Jewish country, the surrounding Arab nations would start a new war. As a result, Jewish survivors all over the world started fund drives to buy arms for settlers. It was hoped that everyone would donate 50 percent of their belongings for this cause.

UN DECLARES ISRAEL THE JEWISH HOMELAND

By the end of April 1948, the UN, with a majority vote, gave the Jews the homeland they had longed for. At the same time, all the Jews held by the British on Cyprus were allowed to leave for the new State of Israel. Among them was Symcha and Ethel's son, Alter. When they arrived in Israel, most were faced with the immediate task of defending the young country. Alter was selected to learn how to plant land mines against the approaching Egyptian tanks. Tragically, however, while trying to plant a defective land mine, it exploded and he was killed. He was not quite twenty years of age.

When the news of Alter's death reached the family in Landshut, Symcha, Ethel, and Sarah left immediately for Israel, to be with their younger son, Sam. A few months later, we received a letter from Symcha advising us not to come to Israel at that time since there was not enough housing. His family was still living in a tent camp and the economy in the young country was quite poor.

PASSING THE STATUE OF LIBERTY: FINALLY, AMERICA IN SIGHT

In May of 1949, Sam and Stefa were called to the American Consulate and told to get ready to leave for the US. As soon as he arrived, he sent us a letter stating that he saw great opportunities for all of us in the United States.

Two months later, the rest of us received word that the time had come for us to get ready for our trip to America.

First, we had to go to a city named Amberg, where we went through blood tests and X-rays. From there, we went by truck to Wildflecken where we had to remain for a short time. Our next stop was in Bremenhafen, a port city, where we boarded a US troop carrier named the General Heinselman.

For some reason, Mendel and Edzia did not get on that particular ship. We left port aboard the 17,000-ton ship on August 3. After a short time, the ship began to shake and we all became ill. After a very unpleasant cruise, we finally passed the Statue of Liberty on August 14, docking at the Port of Brooklyn.

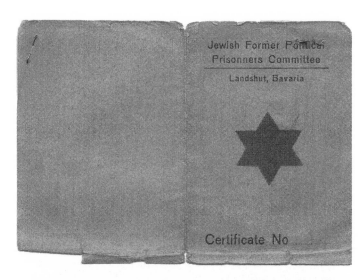

Nathan Berman's ID card, Landshut Bavaria, Germany

Landshut Bavaria, Germany, 1946
Top left to right: Mira Berman, Rena Berman
Bottom left to right: Stefa Berman, Edja Berman, Ethel Berman, Fay Radzinski

Landshut Bavaria, Germany, 1946
Family Reunion Landshut Bavaria, Germany
Top left to right: Frank Radzinski, Sam Berman, Joseph Berman, Rena Berman, Mendel
Berman, Edja Berman, Symcha Berman, Beril Bruer
Middle row left to right: Stefa Berman, Mira Berman, Fay Berman, Nathan Berman, Sarah
Berman, Ethel Berman
Bottom row left to right: Paula Kornblum Popowski, Hannah Kornblum Rushetzky

Soccer Club Landshut Bavaria, Germany, 1947
Nathan Berman, second from top left
Joseph Berman, fifth from top left
Frank Radzinski, second from right
Sam Berman, bottom left

Alter Berman (son of Symcha and Ethel) arrives in Israel 1948

One of two tombstones which survived Kaluszyn cemetery destruction, 2017

One of two tombstones which survived Kaluszyn cemetery destruction
Displayed outside a Catholic church, Kaluszyn, 2017

Original home of Alter Pinchus Berman, Kaluszyn, 2017

Mezuzah backing found in Alter Pinchus Berman's front door entrance

Cemetery Memorial created by Israeli artist, Ken Goldman, Kaluszyn, 2017

EPILOGUE

HAVING ENDURED SOME OF THE WORST HORRORS imaginable, the surviving Bermans would now begin new lives in new worlds.

They survived the Holocaust.

Bound by family ties and unbreakable love, five of them managed to stay in contact and alive as a family in the harsh Kaluszyn countryside after leaping from the death train to Treblinka. For nearly three years, they faced incredible dangers and challenges, staying a step ahead of gestapo, SS, German soldiers, Polish bounty hunters, starvation, frigid exposure, gunshots, wounds, typhoid, and more.

Of approximately fifteen surviving Kaluszyn Jews out of more than 8,000 before the war, eleven were members of the Berman family:

- Joseph
- Mendel

- Nathan
- Fay
- Frank (Fay's husband)
- Sam (Nathan's nephew, son of Motel)

They would soon be joined by six more members of the family who escaped and went to Russia during the war:

Symcha; wife, Ethel; sons, Alter and Sam; daughter, Sarah (born on the train back to Poland); and cousin Chaim Gutarsky.

These family members endured their own severe hardships, including banishment to Siberia.

In both groups, all of the Bermans refused to turn on one another or leave anyone behind, regardless.

When family members like Mendel's daughters succumbed to disease, the heartbreak felt by all was soul crushing, even as they faced their own starvation and death, they still felt the love and compassion to deeply mourn such a terrible loss.

The bonds of family were such that losing one felt like losing everything.

Now, as they began new lives in completely new places, they would take with them the chutzpah Nathan would express as:

"Hitler could not kill me, so why should I be afraid?"

Many of the surviving Bermans would eventually make their way to Detroit, where the old world skills learned in making sheepskin coats would launch them on a journey from factory jobs to once again owning a thriving business. This time, they would focus on cutting leather for the seats of automobiles, while making shearling coats on the side.

The family would again enjoy prosperity by working closely together as a team. Strengthened by the tight bonds first shaped in the Kaluszyn shtetl and in the factory—and then forever cemented by helping one another survive the horrors.

Now, they would enjoy a high degree of freedom and peace. They would finally be free to be unfettered entrepreneurs and capitalists with only the normal pressures of intense competition and life's everyday challenges to face—free from the evil monstrosity of the Nazi death machine and the rampant anti-Semitism it spread throughout Europe and beyond.

These people epitomized the passage in the Torah that says, "for though the righteous falls seven times, they do not lie down."

King Solomon, Proverbs 24:16

While we can never fully comprehend the pain they endured, we can learn from them that life is always worth fighting for, regardless of the horror, loss, and pain— regardless of how many times we fall.

WHAT ABOUT TODAY?

While it is healthy for subsequent generations to move on past the emotional trauma of the Holocaust, it is still important to remain vigilant and aware of the forces that enable such things. Pure evil, hate, and scapegoating fueled the Nazi propaganda machine. Those forces did not die out with Hitler.

Today, anti-Semitism is on the rise around the world.

"It's like we have regressed one hundred years."

—*THE WASHINGTON POST*, US, 2018

BERLIN—Jewish life around the world is under attack once again by "classic traditional anti-Semitism," according to a report by an Israeli university released Wednesday.

...In its latest annual, global assessment of anti-Semitic incidents, the Kantor Center for the Study of Contemporary European Jewry at Tel Aviv University concluded that "Europe's largest Jewish communities are experiencing a normalization and mainstreaming of anti-Semitism not seen since the Second World War.

"Anti-Semitism is on the rise here in the US as well."

—THE ANTI-DEFAMATION LEAGUE (ADL), US, 2018

The ADL says incidents of anti-Semitism rose 60 percent in the US between 2016 and 2017.

...Americans are concerned about violence directed against American Jews...

One of the most disturbing recent manifestations of anti-Semitism in the U.S. was the alt right 'Unite the Right' rally in Charlottesville, Virginia, in August 2017, where hundreds of marchers threw Nazi salutes, waved swastika flags and shouted 'Sieg Heil.' The chaotic event ended violently with the death of a counter-protester. Since that rally, ADL has issued numerous reports on those involved in the demonstrations, including many of the major players in white supremacist movement. Center on Extremism researchers identified more than 200 of the estimated 500-600 individuals who showed up to support the anti-Semitic and racist rally.

THE TREE OF LIFE, PITTSBURGH

NOTE: As this was being written, 11 Jewish worshippers were murdered inside a synagogue in Pittsburgh on the Sabbath by an avowed anti-Semite armed with an AR15. Many others were injured, including 4 police officers who rushed into the synagogue to engage the shooter, who was wounded and arrested.

According to the ADL, this was the deadliest attack on Jews in U.S. history.

In social media posts, the shooter said he was enraged by HIAS, the Hebrew Immigrant Aid Society. HIAS was formed in 1881 to aid Jewish refugees. In 1975, the U.S. State Department asked it to assist Vietnamese refugees and since then it has supported refugees of all nationalities. The shooter also said he wanted to kill all Jews.

THE WORLD TURNED ITS BACK ON JEWS

It is a tragic and hard fact that millions of Jewish lives could have been saved if the world did not turn its back on refugees. And the world, including the U.S., did indeed turn its back.

A single instance noted by the Smithsonian:

> ...the United States had a poor track record offering asylum. Most notoriously, in June 1939, the German ocean liner St. Louis and its 937 passengers, almost all Jewish, were turned away from the port of Miami, forcing the ship to return to Europe; more than a quarter died in the Holocaust.

Britain also shunned Jewish refugees. When World War II broke out, Britain halted any emigration of Jewish refugees from Nazi-controlled countries. Even when it became clear the Nazis were going to exterminate the

Jews, Britain allowed a mere 10,000 Jews to find their way into the U.K.

As late as July of 1947, Britain was still aggressively stopping Jews from entering Palestine (Israel). A ship called the Exodus carrying some 4,500 Jewish immigrants, mostly Holocaust survivors, and including some 1,600 children, was boarded by the British in international waters. They killed 3 of the refugees on board and injured another 10. The ship was then turned back to refugee camps in Europe.

And of course, we know from the Berman family story that Symcha's two sons, Alter and Sam, were members of a Zionist youth organization whose goal was to bring all its members to Palestine. They went to a city in Germany called Greifenberg. There they were trained to farm. A few months later, the entire group was smuggled into Italy and later to France. From there, they boarded a large French fishing boat with a Greek crew. Their destination was Palestine.

As they approached the shores near Tel Aviv, British naval cruisers encircled their boat. The Greek crew abandoned ship and left the passengers to fend for themselves. The British towed the fishing boat to the island of Cyprus and left the refugees there.

Sam and Alter eventually made it to Israel. And in 1948, the UN would declare Israel the Jewish homeland, enabling the settlement of many Jews.

The rest of the world also turned its back.

As the Nazi threat rose in the late 1930s, thirty-two European countries met in Évian, France to discuss the Jewish situation. It became clear there would be few if any safe havens for the Jews. The majority refused to loosen any immigration restrictions to save them.

"The world seemed to be divided into two parts—those places where the Jews could not live, and those where they could not enter."

—CHAIM WEIZMANN, FIRST PRESIDENT OF ISRAEL, SAID ABOUT THE 1938 ÉVIAN CONFERENCE

ABOUT THE AUTHOR

HARVY BERMAN worked alongside his family for more than twenty years. Inside the factory's large conference room, mealtime often became story time, and Harvy got to hear firsthand accounts of the stories shared in this book from his uncles and his father. Harvy's quest to share his family's journey began in earnest when he learned of his father's first wife, who'd been killed during the Holocaust. Harvy started piecing together his family's history from before, during, and after that horrific event, and is proud to share it for the first time in *Undying Will*.

APPENDIX

REFERENCES AND RESOURCES

As stated, the stories on the Holocaust are in the authentic voices of Mendel and Joseph Berman, with occasional notes to help provide clarification or perspective.

The following are among the resources used in developing the soccer stories and historical references to Kaluszyn.

Additional stories are quoted from:

The Memorial Book of Kaluszyn, by Shalom Soroka, translated by William Leibner. Tel Aviv, 1961, https://www. jewishgen.org/Yizkor/kaluszyn/kaluszyn.html.

Jewish Virtual Library—Poland Virtual History Tour https://www.jewishvirtuallibrary.org/ poland-virtual-jewish-history-tour

An online resource with a wealth of historical information on Jews throughout time around the world.

POLIN Museum of the History of Polish Jews https://en.wikipedia.org/wiki/POLIN_Museum_of_the_History_of_Polish_Jews

A museum on the site of the former Warsaw Ghetto. The Hebrew word "Polin" in the museum's English name means either "Poland" or "rest here" and relates to a legend about the arrival of the first Jews to Poland.

Timelines and History of Migration—Poland: Jewish Culture in Poland, by Alicja and Magda, http://www.ghs-mh.de/migration/projects/timeline/tl_pl_1.htm.

Migration and European culture, origins of Jews in Poland, ties to both Jewish and Polish culture.

WEDDINGS

Marriage Ceremonies, by Cyrus Adler and M. Grunwald, *Jewish Encyclopedia*, http://www.jewishencyclopedia.com/articles/10434-marriage-ceremonies.

Polish Weddings: Then & Now, Sasha Vasilyuk, *CulturePL*, Jun. 21, 2017, https://culture.pl/en/article/polish-weddings-then-now.

Weddination: http://weddination.com/2016/03/29/ songs-games-must-know-wedding-phrases/

In Ben-Gurion's Polish Hometown, Residents Dance the Hora Ahead of Israel's 70th, by Yaakov Schwartz, *The Times of Israel*, April 16, 2018, https://www.timesofisrael.com/in-ben-gurions-polish-hometown-residents-dance-the-hora-ahead-of-israels-70th/.

Hora (dance), Wikipedia, Last edited April 23, 2019, https://en.wikipedia.org/wiki/Hora.

(dance)

> Although considered traditional, some claim it rose to popularity due to Hora Agadati, named after dancer and choreographer Baruch Agadati and performed for the first time in 1924. It is usually performed to Israeli folk songs, and sometimes to Jewish songs, typically to the music of Hava Nagila.

JEWISH LIFE IN POLAND BEFORE WORLD WAR II

About the Righteous, Yad Vashem: The World Holocaust Memorial Center, http://www.yadvashem.org/righteous/about-the-righteous.html.

The Righteous Among the Nations, honored by Yad

Vashem, are non-Jews who took great risks to save Jews during the Holocaust...

Names of Righteous by Country, Yad Vashem: The World Holocaust Memorial Center, http://www.yadvashem.org/righteous/statistics.html.

Poles and the Jews: How Deep the Guilt? by Adam Michnik, *New York Times*, March 17, 2001, https://www.nytimes.com/2001/03/17/arts/poles-and-the-jews-how-deep-the-guilt.html.

Rescue of Jews by Poles during the Holocaust, Wikipedia, Last edited May 8, 2019, https://en.wikipedia.org/wiki/Rescue_of_Jews_by_Poles_during_the_Holocaust.

Jewish Life in Poland Before the Holocaust, *Facing History and Ourselves*, excerpt from *The Third Reich at War,* by Richard T. Evans, https://www.facinghistory.org/resource-library/resistance-during-holocaust/jewish-life-poland-holocaust.

Polish Jewry Between the *Wars,* by Karen Auerbach, *My Jewish Learning,* https://www.myjewishlearning.com/article/polish-jewry-between-the-wars/.

A wealth of facts and historical perspectives on Jews in Poland during the times between WWI and WWII.

European Jewish Life Before World War II, *Facing History and Ourselves,* https://www.facinghistory.org/ resource-library/teaching-holocaust-and-human-behavior/ european-jewish-life-world-war-ii.

Tremendous resources for facts and perspectives, as well as descriptions on shtetls like Kaluszyn.

Sholem Aleichem: Understanding the Life of Shtetl Jews, video clip, https://www.facinghistory.org/resource-library/ video/sholem-aleichem-understanding-life-shtetl-jews.

Life in the Shtetl—Vishki, a Shtetl in Latvia, https://www. dumes.net/usdin/shtetld.html.

Yidishkeyt ("Jewishness") and menshlikhkeyt ("humanness") were the two major values of the shtetl community around which life centered...

Shtetls: The Life and Death of a Small Town and the World of Polish Jews, Introduction, by Eva Hoffman, Houghton Mifflin Co., 1997, http://www.pbs.org/wgbh// pages/frontline/shtetl/reflections/.

What remains of the Jews of Poland? Mostly traces, echoes and a few monuments; and also sorrow, rage, guilt and denial. There are a few thousand Jews left in Poland today, but the communities they inhabited, their characteristic culture and society, were all destroyed during World War II. Because the extent of the loss was so great—so total— the act of remembering the vanished world has become fraught with painful and acute emotions.

History of the Jews in Poland, Wikipedia, Last edited May 13, 2019, https://en.wikipedia.org/wiki/History_of_the_Jews_in_Poland.

Why Poland Punishes Those Who Accuse It of the Holocaust, Erin Blakemore, *History Stories,* August 31, 2018, https://www.history.com/news/poland-holocaust-law-death-camps.

Poland Since 1939, by David Engel, *Yivo Encyclopedia of Jews in Eastern Europe,* http://www.yivoencyclopedia.org/article.aspx/Poland/Poland_since_1939.

"Kaluszyn," *JewishGen: Encyclopedia of Jewish Communities:* https://www.jewishgen.org/yizkor/pinkas_poland/pol4_00399.html.

From Persecution to Genocide, by David Cesarani, *BBC History,* http://www.bbc.co.uk/history/worldwars/genocide/radicalisation_01.shtml.

WIKI: Jewish Ghettos, https://en.wikipedia.org/wiki/Jewish_ghettos_in_German-occupied_Poland.

By the time Nazi-occupied Eastern Europe was liberated by the Red Army, not a single Jewish ghetto in Poland was left standing. Only about 50,000–120,000 Polish Jews survived the war on native soil with the assistance of their Polish neighbors, a fraction of their prewar population of 3,500,000.

Polish anti-Semitism, http://visegradinsight.eu/the-polish-underground-and-the-jews-1939-1945/.

Points out situation was more complex and diverse than black and white:

> A refreshing antidote is The Polish Underground and the Jews, 1939–1945 by Yeshiva University's Prof. Joshua Zimmerman. This excellent, painstakingly documented work is an effective weapon against biased accounts of this episode in history.

The Crooked Mirror: A Memoir of Polish-Jewish Reconciliation, Kindle Edition, https://www.jewishbookcouncil.org/book/the-crooked-mirror.

Although an estimated 80 percent of American Jews are of Polish descent, many in the postwar generation and those born later know little about their families' connection to their ancestral home.

Here is a snapshot of what Americans were saying about Jews as they sought to escape Hitler's Nazi vise for refuge in the United States.

What Did Americans Say About Jewish Holocaust Refugees? Uriel Heilman, *Haaretz*, December 3, 2015, https://www.haaretz.com/jewish/what-did-americans-say-about-jewish-refugees-1.5430021.

HAARETZ, Israel, 2018 TA—They were called "so-called" refugees, told they were alien to American culture and warned against as potential enemies of the United States.

This heated anti-refugee rhetoric in America was directed against Jews trying to flee Europe, not Mexicans or Syrians. Back in the 1930s and '40s, the fear was of Nazi and Communist infiltrators sneaking in along with the refugees rather than the ISIS militants or Mexican criminals that some fear today.

"Try to keep them out."

In 1938, when Hitler's threat to Jews in Germany already was apparent, America still was emerging from the Great Depression, and xenophobia and anti-Semitism were commonplace. In a July 1938 poll, 67 percent of Americans told *Fortune* magazine that America should try to keep out altogether German, Austrian, and other political refugees, and another 18 percent said America should allow them in, but without increasing immigration quotas. In another 1938 poll, cited in the book *Jews in the Mind of America*, some 75 percent of respondents said they opposed increasing the number of German Jews allowed to resettle in the United States.

In January 1939, 61 percent of Americans told Gallup they opposed the settlement of 10,000 refugee children, "most of them Jewish," in the United States.

3 Things We've Learned Since Last Year's World Refugee Day, by Madelieine Ngo, *Vox,* The United Nations, 2018 https://www.vox.com/world/2018/6/20/17479612/world-refugee-day-immigration-venezuela.

The UN defines a refugee as "someone who has been forced to flee his or her country because of persecution, war, or violence..."

The number of displaced people in the world has never been higher.

By the end of last year, according to a recent UNHCR report, there were 68.5 million forcibly displaced people in the world, including 25.4 million refugees. The number also includes about 40 million internally displaced people—

people who were forced to leave their homes but are still in their home countries—and 3.1 million asylum seekers, or people who have applied for refugee status, but are waiting for approval.

Refugees, *Holocaust Encyclopedia,* United States Memorial Holocaust Museum https://encyclopedia.ushmm.org/content/en/article/refugees.

After Germany annexed Austria in March 1938 and particularly after the Kristallnachtpogroms of November 9-10, 1938, nations in western Europe and the Americas feared an influx of refugees.

About 85,000 Jewish refugees (out of 120,000 Jewish emigrants) reached the United States between March 1938 and September 1939, but this level of immigration was far below the number seeking refuge. In late 1938, 125,000 applicants lined up outside US consulates hoping to obtain 27,000 visas under the existing immigration quota. By June 1939, the number of applicants had increased to over 300,000. Most visa applicants were unsuccessful. At the Évian Conference in July 1938, only the Dominican Republic stated that it was prepared to admit significant numbers of refugees, although Bolivia would admit around 30,000 Jewish immigrants between 1938 and 1941.

The U.S. Government Turned Away Thousands of Jewish

Refugees, Fearing That They Were Nazi Spies, by Daniel A. Gross, *Smithsonian.com*, November 18, 2015, Smithsonian. com 2015 https://www.smithsonianmag. com/history/ us-government-turned-away-thousands-jewish-refugees-fearing-they-were-nazi-spies-180957324/.

World War II prompted the largest displacement of human beings the world had ever seen—although today's refugee crisis is starting to approach its unprecedented scale. But lions of European Jews displaced from their homes, the United States had a poor track record offering asylum. Most notoriously, in June 1939, the German ocean liner St. Louis and its 937 passengers, almost all Jewish, were turned away from the port of Miami, forcing the ship to return to Europe; more than a quarter died in the Holocaust." Read more:

Jews Escaping from German-occupied Europe to the United Kingdom, Wikipedia, Last edited April 2, 2019, https://en.wikipedia.org/wiki/Jews_escaping_from_German-occupied_Europe_to_the_United_Kingdom.

Realizing a plan was needed to manage the large number of emigrants from Nazi Europe, thirty-two countries met in France at the Évian Conference (July 1938), but almost all of them would not loosen their immigration restrictions to take in more refugees. Although the numbers were limited, Britain eased its policy for refugees after

Kristallnacht (the Night of Broken Glass) in Germany on 9 November 1938. On that night, Jewish establishments were vandalized during protests, resulting in broken windows, damaged businesses, and burned synagogues. By September 1939, 70,000 or more than 80,000 Jewish refugees were accepted in Britain. Most of the people settled in North West London.

There were more than 500,000 case files, though, of Jews who were not admitted according to British Jewish associations. Louise London, author of *Whitehall And The Jews*, 1933–1948, stated that "The (British immigration) process... was designed to keep out large numbers of European Jews— perhaps ten times as many as it let in.

When World War II was declared (September 1, 1939), Britain no longer allowed emigration from Nazi-controlled countries. There were also no plans to manage the refugee crisis as the result of the Bermuda Conference of the Allies in April 1943, by which time it was known that the Nazi regime intended to exterminate all of the Jews in Europe (the plan known as the Final Solution). There were 10,000 Jewish refugees who "managed to find their way into Britain" throughout the war (1939–1945).

Britain did not allow Jews to immigrate to Palestine, which was under British control at that time. Even so, there were some Jews who illegally immigrated (Aliyah Bet) to Palestine.

SOCCER

Bela Sebestyen, *Wikipedia*, Last updated March 28, 2018, https://en.wikipedia.org/ wiki/B%C3%A9la_Sebesty%C3%A9n.

Sebestyen was considered one of the greatest wingers in Hungary's early soccer history. He appeared in 24 international games for the National Team between 1906–1912. According to Andrew Handler in *From the Ghetto to the Games*, Bela possessed 'lightning speed, imaginative dribbling, and accurate passing...(he) terrorized the defense for opponents.' Sebestyen was also known for being an exceedingly unselfish player. During his international career, Bela scored only two goals because he preferred to allow his talented teammates to enjoy the glory of scoring.

One of the best wingers in Hungary in the 1900s and 1910s, Sebestyen played for the club team MTK Budapest. He played with the first team, but only won a single Hungarian League Championship (1908). During this time, he also appeared with the Hungarian National team 24 times. In 1912, Bela was a starter on Hungary's Olympic team. They finished in fifth place.

List of Jewish Footballers: https://en.wikipedia.org/wiki/ List_of_Jewish_footballers (Click "Date of Birth" to show Born in 1800s).

The Strategies + Ideals Behind Defending As A Team: Teamwork & Communication, *Coach Up Nation*, August 25, 2016, https://www.coachup.com/nation/articles/ complete-defending.

Soccer Tips for Playing Better Defense, *Active,* https://www.active.com/soccer/articles/ soccer-tips-for-playing-better-defense.

How to Defend in Soccer, *The Compete Soccer Guide,* March 8, 2016, https://www.completesoccerguide.com/ soccer-defending/.

How to Defend Against Fast Attackers, video, *Online Soccer Academy*, https://www.youtube.com/ watch?v=t4hyW_35O6k.

10861750R00169

Made in the USA
Monee, IL
02 September 2019